# GLORIFY

# GLORIFY

A Devotional thorugh the Gospel of John
to Encourage You to Know and Honor Christ

# Joel Engle

## with Pat Springle

Published by Baxter Press, Friendswood, Texas

Printed in the United States of America

Cover illustration by Aaron McClung, Euless, Texas
Cover layout by John Gilmore, Gilmore Marketing, Houston, Texas

ISBN: 1-888237-27-9

# Word and Song

Over the past several months, God has been making me much more aware of his presence. I am beginning to see his hand at work in my conversations with people, in delays in my schedule, and in times when I normally haven't even thought about God at all. Even though I feel like I am barely pulling back the curtain to see God at work, it's really exciting!

I wanted to write this devotional to share with you some of the things Jesus is doing in my life. These pages focus on the Gospel of John, and they point us to an experience each day of the wonderful presence of Christ. Sometimes his presence affirms the direction we are headed; sometimes he changes our direction. But always he communicates his great love to us.

## How to use this devotional:

This devotional correlates to the songs on the CD, Glorify. Some days you will use a song to praise God, and some days you will use a song to think, reflect, and pray. Each day's devotion contains a passage from John and some thoughts about that passage. So, for each day. . . .

—First, read the passage of Scripture at the top of the page,
—Second, read the devotional thought,
—Third, use the prayer-starter to talk to God about what you've read,
—Fourth, take the step to apply what you've learned, and

If you read the passage listed at the bottom of each page, you will have read the whole Gospel of John by the time you finish the book. Cool, huh?!

At the end of each week are some questions to help you think about the last few days and see what Christ is doing in your life. These questions can also be really helpful to get group discussion off the ground.

I hope God will use this devotional and the songs on the CD to help you:
—experience the Lord's presence,
—soak in the truth,
—be a student of the Word, and
—put your faith into action.

Every time you listen to a song on the CD or read a devotional, say, "Jesus, I'm here, and I'm listening. Speak to my heart." He will. It is my prayer that the truth of the Scriptures and the praise of the songs will encourage your faith a lot.

Your friend,

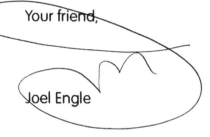

Joel Engle

# I'VE FOUND JESUS

Well I hear they're dancin' in the street 'cause
Jesus is alive
And all creation shouts aloud that
Jesus is alive
Now surely we can all be changed 'cause
Jesus is alive
And everybody here can know that
Jesus is alive

And I will live for all my days
To raise a banner of truth and life
To sing about my Savior's love
And the best thing that happened
Was the day I met You

I've found Jesus, I've found Jesus
I've found Jesus, I've found Jesus

Well  I feel like dancin' in the street 'cause
Jesus is alive
To join with all who celebrate that
Jesus is alive!
Well the joy of God is in this town 'cause
Jesus is alive
For everybody's seen the truth that
Jesus is alive

# Day 1   I'm Listening, Lord

> In the beginning was the Word, and the Word was with God, and the Word was God. (John 1:1)

In the very first sentence of John's gospel, he says two important things about Jesus: He identifies him as the eternal, all-knowing, all-powerful God, and he indicates that Christ is the Father's most important way of communicating to you and me. Jesus is called "the Word."

God communicates to us in several ways: always through the Scriptures, but also sometimes through circumstances, through the words of people, and through impressions as we pray. And occasionally, God breaks into our thoughts and directly shares his heart with us.

Throughout the pages of the Bible and in every period of history, God spoke to men and women . . . sometimes in audible words, most often in the stillness of their hearts. And he wants to do the same thing with you and me. The question is, are we listening? When we read the Bible (or this devotional), are we just checking it off our spiritual to-do list, or are we expecting the one who loves us to speak to us? When we pray, do we go through our many requests and get it over with so we can get on with other (more important?) things, or do we take time to listen to the Spirit of God and let him direct our prayers? And when we sit in class, talk with friends, drive to the mall, or do the zillion other things we do every day, are we aware that we are in the presence of God, and that he may—he just may—want to give us hope or direction or a word of caution?

 Jesus, forgive me for being too busy—or too preoccupied—to listen to you. Help me tune in to you more often.

Ask the Lord to remind you of messages he has communicated to you in the past. And listen.

Read John 1:1-14

# Grace and Truth

> For the law was given through Moses; grace and truth came through Jesus Christ. (John 1:17)

And what is the message Jesus wants us to hear? Grace and truth. In the first century, that was a revolutionary message! It still is today. Moses' law—The Ten Commandments—gave instructions about how to please God. Some of them covered the externals: don't murder, don't commit adultery, and sins like that. But other commands dealt with the heart: don't desire anything owned by somebody else, love God with all your heart, and never ever say or do anything against your parents. The Jewish people didn't stop with those ten. They came up with hundreds more rules to live by. The problem is that nobody in the world (except Jesus) could ever do them all perfectly. It's impossible! And because perfection is impossible for us, the rules show us how much we need a Savior.

Grace doesn't say, "Oh, don't worry about your sins. They're no big deal." No, grace is coupled with truth, the hard truth that our sins stink in God's nostrils. Truth comes when the Holy Spirit taps me on the shoulder and says, "You know, that was wrong. It was sin. You need to repent." Grace is the incredible forgiveness of God to wash away the sin and to make us whole.

Some of us have done some really awful things, but the grace of God is bigger and more wonderful than we can imagine. Others of us try to earn God's acceptance by keeping our own version of the law. We go to every youth group function; we pray; we read the Bible every day—we've done so much that we feel God owes us! The grace of God even covers that self-righteous sin, too. Grace and truth: Bigger than our sin. Better than we can imagine.

 Jesus, when you make me aware of my sins, I am even more thankful for your grace.

Listen to "I've Found Jesus." Think about God's grace to you as you listen.

Read John 1:15-34

# Excited!

> Andrew, Simon Peter's brother, was one of the two who heard what John had said and who had followed Jesus. The first thing Andrew did was to find his brother Simon and tell him, "We have found the Messiah" (that is, the Christ). And he brought him to Jesus. (John 1:40-42a)

A friend of mine found a folded $50 bill on the sidewalk of a busy street. At first, he couldn't believe his eyes. He picked it up and looked around to see if any of the hundreds of people walking by would stop and look for it. The crowd kept streaming by. Nobody else in the world seemed to notice. He hurried to a restaurant to meet a friend, and as soon as they saw each other, he excitedly blurted out his discovery.

I think that's exactly how Andrew felt when he found Jesus and then hurried to tell his brother the good news about what (or who) he'd found. Sometimes we are afraid to tell people about Jesus. We're afraid they'll make fun of us, or they might ask us really hard questions about our faith. If we camp on those fears long enough, the joy of finding Jesus gradually fades until it is no more exciting than finding a good movie. Or even less.

Andrew knew he had found the greatest treasure anyone could possibly find: forgiveness, peace, and purpose . . . through a strong, loving Savior. Nothing could contain his excitement! In the pages of the gospels, we see Andrew again and again bringing people to Jesus. We don't see him standing on a hill or in a synagogue preaching; we don't see him arguing fine points with religious leaders. That wasn't his style of evangelism. He simply told people, "Hey, come with me! You gotta meet this guy! He's terrific!"

Let the joy of being loved and forgiven fill your heart, and then tell somebody, "Hey, you gotta meet this guy!" That's what evangelism is all about.

Jesus, you are the greatest treasure I could ever find. Thank you for loving me, for forgiving me, and for giving me something to live for.

Invite someone to your youth group, Bible study, or Christian group on campus.

Read John 1:35-42

# He Knows All

When Jesus saw Nathanael approaching, he said of him, "Here is a true Israelite, in whom there is nothing false."

"How do you know me?" Nathanael asked.

Jesus answered, "I saw you while you were still under the fig tree before Philip called you."

Then Nathanael declared, "Rabbi, you are the Son of God; you are the King of Israel." (John 1:47-49)

Nathanael was an honest skeptic, not a cynic. When Philip told him he had found the Messiah, Nathanael wanted some kind of confirmation so he could believe it was true. As Nathanael walked toward Jesus, I have a sneaking suspicion that Jesus had a smile on his face. He knew Nathanael didn't believe easily, but he also knew that he had a good and honest heart. Jesus' words showed Nathanael that Jesus saw into his heart, and that Jesus knew what no ordinary man could know about him: who he was, what he had done, and where he had been.

Jesus is still smiling as he speaks to honest skeptics—like you and me. He speaks his words to us through the Scriptures and through the Spirit to tell us, "I know all about you. I know your hopes and your fears. And I know every single thing you've ever done—yes, even that. And I love you anyway."

It can be a scary thing to realize that Jesus knows absolutely everything about us, but with that insight comes his smile. He knows . . . and he forgives. He knows . . . and he cares. He knows . . . and he never turns his back on us. That's why Nathanael embraced Christ with all his heart.

That's why we can, too.

 Lord Jesus, you know everything about me, and you still smile. Thank you for not turning your back or turning up your nose at me. Thank you for caring.

☞ Write the letters JK and JC on your thumb. Every time you see them today, remember that: "Jesus knows. Jesus cares." Be prepared to respond when people ask, "What are those letters on your hand?"

Read John 1:43-51

# Day 5   Behind the Scenes

> Jesus said to the servants, "Fill the jars with water"; so they filled them to the brim. Then he told them, "Now draw some out and take it to the master of the banquet." They did so, and the master of the banquet tasted the water that had been turned into wine. He did not realize where it had come from, though the servants who had drawn the water knew. (John 2:7-9a)

A miracle had happened—but only a few people knew about it. Most of the people at the banquet kept eating and drinking without a clue that heaven had visited their party. Who knew? Only the servants.

I suspect that this same thing happens again and again in our lives: Behind the scenes, God is actively at work accomplishing his purposes, changing hearts, and orchestrating circumstances, but most of us are clueless. Only the servants know.

I want to be one of the servants. I want to be one of those people Jesus comes to and say, "Do you have a few minutes? I want you to help me with this miracle." Then, as he gives instructions, I simply do what he says and watch him work.

Those servants might have wondered, "What is this guy up to? Why in the world would he ask us to fill these jars with water in the middle of a party? This is a waste of time." If they had refused to do what Jesus said, they would have missed the thrill of their lives.

Jesus is looking for servants today who are willing to do what he says and watch him work miracles. Yeah, we may think what he asks us to do is crazy, but if we follow through, we will see him at work like never before.

Who do you think was giving each other high fives at that party? The people at the banquet? No, they were clueless. The servants and Jesus were laughing and celebrating. They had seen a miracle.

 Lord Jesus, I want to be a servant behind the scenes with you—not just a guest at the party.

☞ Today, look behind the scenes (at school, in your youth group, in your family) to see what God is really up to.

Read John 2:1-11

# End of the Week

## Looking up:

Listen to "I've Found Jesus." What are evidences in your life that "Jesus is alive"?

## Looking back:

1. Which day's devotion and passage of Scripture meant the most to you this week? Explain:

2. How has God made his presence known to you (in your prayers, study of the Scriptures, in quiet moments, busy times, and in conversations)?

3. How have you seen God's hand at work in your circumstances and in the lives of others this week?

4. How have you responded to temptation, and what help did you find at the most difficult moments?

5. What fruit of the Spirit (Galatians 5:22-23) would you like to see increase in your life? (Love, Joy, Peace, Patience, Kindness, Goodness, Gentleness, Faithfulness, Self-control) What difference would this make in your attitude, relationships, etc?

6. What opportunities has God given you to serve others, and how did you respond?

7. Did God provide an opportunity for you to share your faith with someone? What happened?

8. As you look to next week, what are some good choices you need to make?

In order to make those choices, Lord, I need you to. . . .

# EVERY MOVE I MAKE

Every move I make I make in You
You make me move Jesus
Every breath I take I breathe in You
Every step I take I take in You
You are my way Jesus
Every breath I take I breathe in You

Na na na-na-na-na
Na-na na na-na-na-na-na

You are holy, Lord
You are holy, Lord
I worship You
You are holy, Lord
You are holy, Lord
I worship You     I worship You

Waves of mercy, waves of grace
Everywhere I look I see Your face
Your love has captured me
Oh my God, this love, how can it be

# Day 1 Hacked Off—Reasonably

So he made a whip out of cords, and drove all from the temple area, both sheep and cattle; he scattered the coins of the money changers and overturned their tables. To those who sold doves he said, "Get these out of here! How dare you turn my Father's house into a market!" (John 2:15-16)

Jesus was hacked off—really hacked off! No, he wasn't out of control. He was very much in control of his behavior. His anger and his actions were carefully calculated to defend the glory of God.

In our day, tolerance is taught as the supreme social gospel in our schools. We are told that we should accept each person's beliefs because they are all of equal value. But that means there is no truth to anchor our lives, no standard for right and wrong.

We have to be careful about anger. Most of the time, it is based on selfishness, jealousy, and envy. But as we walk with God and understand his purposes for people, we will become angry about the things he is angry about: injustice, abuse, and devaluing people. It is good and right to be angry (controlled, measured, and reasoned) about schools and government supporting abortion and homosexual lifestyles. It is also right to stand strong against tolerance because it tries to undermine the foundations of faith. But we should also be indignant about the way many movies and television shows make fun of people, laugh at sin, and try to amuse us with senseless violence, sex, and profanity.

How do you think Jesus would respond to these things? What would he say in class when tolerance is preached? What stand would he take on homosexuality? And what would he say about many of the movies our friends (and we?) watch "because there's nothing better to do"?

Jesus, give me your perspective on things that make you angry. Help me to be angry about the right things, and then to act in an appropriate, reasoned way to show that anger.

Look at a list of movies showing today. What values (good or bad) do they communicate? Think about how Jesus would respond to each of them.

Read John 2: 12-17

> After he was raised from the dead, his disciples recalled what he had said. Then they believed the Scripture and the words that Jesus had spoken. (John 2:22)

This passage encourages me. The disciples were with Jesus all day every day, but they still didn't understand a lot of things. They were just like me!

Jesus told them over and over again that he was going to be killed and then raised from the dead. Maybe the disciples didn't want that to happen to Jesus, so they refused to listen. Or maybe they realized that if Jesus was killed, they (gulp!) would probably be killed, too. For whatever reason, they didn't get it. It was only after Jesus was raised from the dead that the lights went on.

That happens with me, too. The Scriptures tell me over and over again that God is in control, he cares, and I can trust him. Still, I worry about all kinds of things. But after the storm has passed, I can look back and realize that God was at work through it all. He really was in control. He showed he cared, and I could have trusted him.

Jesus was very patient with his disciples, and I'm really glad he's patient with me, too. He gently reminds me, "See, I told you I was on top of things. You worried for no reason at all. Maybe next time. . . ."

Yeah, maybe next time.

God wants us to look back from time to time to see his hand at work in our lives. We may not be able to see it in the middle of the storm, but if we look back often enough, maybe that will give us enough confidence that we will be able to trust him in the middle of the storm next time.

Maybe.

 Jesus, when I look back I can see your hand at work. . . .

☞ Listen to "Every Move I Make."

Read John 2:18-25

# Day 3 See His Smile

> "For God did not send his Son into the world to condemn the world, but to save the world through him." (John 3:17)

When you think of Jesus, what expression do you imagine on his face as he looks at you? Scowling? Disappointed? Disgusted? Or warm and loving?

The expression we envision on his face determines how we relate to him. If we think he is condemning, then we will either try all day every day to do everything we can do to please him—but we'll never feel that we've done enough. Or we'll give up and walk away from him. We may hang around Christians because they are nice to us, but we will avoid any real interaction with Jesus. It hurts too bad to be scowled at.

But the good news is that he doesn't scowl at us! He didn't come to condemn the world. He could have done that from a zillion miles out in space and zapped us all back to the Big Bang! No, Jesus stepped out of eternity into time and space to show how much he loves you and me. No matter what awful thing you've done, he reaches out his hand to you. No matter how rigid and self-righteous you are, his smile can melt your fearful heart.

Think of Jesus. See a smile.

 Lord Jesus, thank you for looking through my sin and seeing me. Help me see your smile.

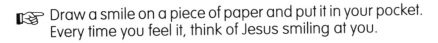 Draw a smile on a piece of paper and put it in your pocket. Every time you feel it, think of Jesus smiling at you.

Read John 3:1-18

# Let the Light Shine

> "Every one who does evil hates the light, and will not come into the light for fear that his deeds will be exposed. But whoever lives by the truth comes into the light. . . ." (John 3:20-21)

When I think of evil and darkness, I usually think of the most wicked sins. Don't you? But as I think of how people who responded to Jesus, I am struck with the realization of who came to Jesus and who feared him. Over and over again in the Scriptures, Jesus is approached by despised prostitutes, by hated tax collectors who made money off their own people, by people who were diseased, and by those who were possessed by demons. It's hard to get darker than that! Yet these people were drawn to the Light, and they were transformed by the power of his love and truth.

And who feared the light? Who despised Jesus and condemned him? The self-righteous religious leaders. They wanted to keep their spirituality boxed into a set of rigid rules. They wanted no part of forgiveness, love, and joy.

After we have been Christians for a while, it is easy to gradually lose the thrill of our salvation and slip into the darkness of defining our Christian lives by what we don't do. Don't let that happen to you! Let the light shine on your heart. Have the courage to be ruthlessly honest about your sins (especially the self-righteous ones), and enjoy the incredible excitement of walking in Jesus' love.

 Lord, your light makes me feel. . . .

 Is there evidence of self-righteous rules in your life? If there is, ask God to give you a fresh thankfulness for his grace and your forgiveness—and the freedom to enjoy walking with him.

Read John 3:19-21

# Day 5      Big Steps

"He must become greater; I must become less."—John the Baptist (John 3:30)

This statement by John the Baptist is one of the hallmarks of Christian growth. As we grow in our faith, Jesus' purposes, presence, and power become more and more evident in our lives. We care more about his reputation than our own. We want to speak his words instead of babbling our own. This process happens in two ways: one is easy; the other is very hard.

The easy part occurs as we experience more and more of God's great love. Like a couple in love, we want other people to know how wonderful that other one is to us. And we want to know that person as deeply as possible. As we respond to Jesus' love, we quite naturally want to please him in every way possible.

But as we grow closer to Jesus, the light of his presence shines on the deepest parts of our lives: pet sins we excuse, secret desires we don't want to let go of, treasured possessions, special people who occupy too much of our hearts. The Lord gently taps us on the shoulder and says, "Do you see this? It's in the way of my purposes for you. I love you too much to ignore it any longer. Take it out of the center of your heart."

Ouch! These are some of the hardest times of our spiritual experience, but they are also times of our greatest growth. Many people quit right here. Don't misunderstand me: All of us hesitate at this point. It's only natural. But the courageous will nod and say, "Yes, Lord. Help me put you first." And that person takes a giant step of spiritual growth.

 Lord, you have shined your light on this idol in my heart:

☞ Listen to "Every Move I Make" and make it your prayer.

Read John 3:22-36

# THE LORD LIVETH

I will call upon the Lord
Who is worthy to be praised
So shall I be saved from my enemies
I will call upon the Lord

The Lord liveth
And blessed be the rock
And let the God of our salvation
be exalted

The Lord liveth
And blessed be the rock
And let the God of our salvation
be exalted

# End of the Week

## Looking up:

Listen to "The Lord Liveth" and think about how the song's message is real in your life.

## Looking back:

1. Which day's devotion and passage of Scripture meant the most to you this week? Explain:

2. How has God made his presence known to you (in your prayers, study of the Scriptures, in quiet moments, busy times, and in conversations)?

3. How have you seen God's hand at work in your circumstances and in the lives of others this week?

4. How have you responded to temptation, and what help did you find at the most difficult moments?

5. What fruit of the Spirit (Galatians 5:22-23) would you like to see increase in your life? (Love, Joy, Peace, Patience, Kindness, Goodness, Gentleness, Faithfulness, Self-control) What difference would this make in your attitude, relationships, etc?

6. What opportunities has God given you to serve others, and how did you respond?

7. Did God provide an opportunity for you to share your faith with someone? What happened?

8. As you look to next week, what are some good choices you need to make?

In order to make those choices, Lord, I need you to. . . .

# OPEN THE EYES OF MY HEART

Open the eyes of my heart, Lord
Open the eyes of my heart
I want to see You, I want to see You

Open the eyes of my heart, Lord
Open the eyes of my heart
I want to see You, I want to see You

To see You, high and  lifted up
Shining in the light of Your glory
Pour out Your power and love
As we cry holy, holy, holy

Holy, holy, holy
Holy, holy, holy
Holy, holy, holy
I want to see You

# Day 1 Break the Rules——Reach Out

> When a Samaritan woman came to draw water, Jesus said to her, "Will you give me a drink?"
>
> The Samaritan woman said to him, "You are a Jew and I am a Samaritan woman. How can you ask me for a drink?" (For Jews do not associate with Samaritans.) (John 4:7-9)

Jesus broke all the rules. Jews weren't supposed to have anything to do with the despised Samaritans, but Jesus went to them. Men weren't supposed to speak to women outside their families, but Jesus initiated a conversation. Jesus didn't care about the social rules; he only cared about people. He often caught flak for spending time with outcasts. That was a price he was more than willing to pay for the opportunity to let people respond to his love for them.

Who are the Samaritans in your school? . . . in your neighborhood? . . . in your city? . . . in your family? Who are the ones that people avoid because they have a different skin color, or speak with an accent, or dress differently, or act strangely?

Reach out to these people, but don't use a "hit and run" approach. Take time to show you care. Share your heart. And listen. Really listen. Learn to see those people as just as valuable as you are to God. They'll know if you are spending time with them only because you "ought to" or because you really care.

They'll know you care if you listen.

 Lord Jesus, as I read these words, I thought of _____. Give me the grace to be a friend to these people. And the grace to listen.

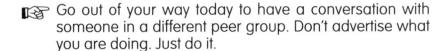 Go out of your way today to have a conversation with someone in a different peer group. Don't advertise what you are doing. Just do it.

Read John 4:1-26

# Feeling Full

"My food," said Jesus, "is to do the will of him who sent me and to finish his work." (John 4:34)

Jesus was so consumed with his purpose to minister to others that he didn't even notice when he was hungry. What filled him up, he told his disciples, was the thrill of watching his Father work through him.

Nothing else comes close.

Philosopher Blaise Paschal said, "There is a God-shaped vacuum in the heart of each man (and woman) which cannot be filled by any created thing, but only by God, the Creator, made known through Jesus Christ." We can try to fill that hole with possessions, people, and prestige, but these soon leave us feeling just as empty as before. We long for God to fill us, and we are not satisfied until we "know the love of Christ which surpasses knowledge." (Eph 3:19)

Where does this consuming desire to do God's will come from? From God. Pastor A. W. Tozer wrote, "We pursue God because, and only because, he has first put an urge within us that spurs us to the pursuit."

So great is the grace of God that he initiates our desire to know him, he reveals himself to us at our slightest response, and then he confirms his love and power to us in thousands of acts of his mercy, strength, and goodness as we try to obey him! That's the adventure of knowing and serving God. That's what really satisfies.

 Jesus, fan the flame of desire in my heart to know and obey you more than ever before.

 Listen to "Open the Eyes of My Heart." What does it mean to "see Jesus"?

Read John 4:27-34

# Day 3    Eyes on the Harvest

> "Do you not say, 'Four months more and then the harvest'? I tell you, open your eyes and look at the fields! They are ripe for harvest." (John 4:35)

Jesus had a revolutionary perspective about people. His disciples couldn't understand why in the world he had stopped to talk to a Samaritan woman—who was little more than a prostitute!

But where the disciples saw sin, Jesus saw pain. Where the disciples saw a bad person, Jesus saw someone who was ready to respond to his love. Where the disciples saw hopelessness, Jesus saw an opening for the grace of God to change a life.

Same person. Two completely different perspectives of her.

Walk down the hall of your school during a class break. What do you see? Go to  the mall in the late afternoon. What do you see there? Do you see faceless, nameless people who are clogging up the walkways, or do you see individuals whose hopes and dreams, fears and hurts make them open to God's Spirit speaking to them.

I know a pastor who is so overwhelmed with the grace of God that he talks to every person he can find about Jesus. And he is genuinely surprised when somebody doesn't embrace Christ. He sees the fields as ripe for harvest, and he is really glad to work in those fields!

 Lord, help me see people with your eyes, to see their pain as an opportunity to tell them about the greatest love they can ever imagine. And give me the courage to tell them.

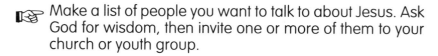 Make a list of people you want to talk to about Jesus. Ask God for wisdom, then invite one or more of them to your church or youth group.

Read John 4:35-42

> Jesus replied, "You may go. Your son will live."
> The man took Jesus at his word. . . . (John 4:50)

The Bible is a huge book. HUGE! If you thumb through it and glance at the pages, it's easy to get confused by all the kings and wars and crazy events in the Old Testament. A lot of that is history, and it takes some time to understand, but by the time we get to the gospels and the rest of the New Testament, the meaning is usually much clearer. In fact, the truths in the Scriptures are the clearest and best road map we can have for a rich, meaningful life!

But to have that kind of life, we have to take Jesus at his word.

The Bible is both a love letter and an instruction manual. In its pages, we find the incredible message that the God of the Universe stepped out of heaven to rescue us from eternal death. He loves us so much that he calls us his friends. And in these pages, we get clear direction about how God wants us to live—not to ruin our fun, but to make our lives as rich as possible.

The Bible contains facts (about God, about history, and things like that), commands (to keep us on the right road), and promises (to give us encouragement and hope). In fact, Peter calls them "precious and magnificent promises," such as: God will always provide, his timing is always right, he will never leave us, and he will always forgive us and give us strength to do what's right.

His message is clear. The question is: are we willing to take Jesus at his word?

 Jesus, the messages of your love and your promises are clear. I need to know them better so I can take you at your word.

 As you read your Bible, mark "F" for facts, "C" for commands, and "P" for promises you find.

Read John 4:43-54

# Day 5     Always at Work

Jesus said to them, "My Father is always at his work to this very day, and I, too, am working." (John 5:17)

Professor and author Dallas Willard says we live in a "God-bathed world." He explains that God is actively and intentionally involved in every person's life at every minute. Sometimes we are aware of his presence. Most of the time, we are clueless.

Wouldn't it be exciting to be aware of God's Spirit speaking to us each day and to watch his hand at work in people's lives—including ours? The problem is not that God isn't there. The problem is that we need to tune in on his frequency. Here's how you can tune in better:

—Expect to find God. The Scriptures clearly teach that God wants to communicate to you and me. Believe it.

—Study the Scriptures. The Bible tells us about God's heart and his ways. As we read and study, we will learn what to look and listen for.

—Reflect. Take time to be quiet so you can think about a passage of Scripture you have read or an impression the Spirit has given you. As you become more reflective, you will also become aware of God's leading in the middle of activities and conversations.

—Hang out with people who believe that God is at work all around them. Learn from these people.

—Obey the Lord. As you make choices to follow God's leading, you will be even more in tune with him. But if you refuse, the signal gets a little fuzzy until you come around.

God is not distant. He's right here with you. Become aware of his powerful presence.

 Lord, help me be aware of your presence with me and around me today.

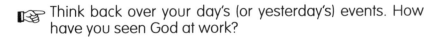 Think back over your day's (or yesterday's) events. How have you seen God at work?

Read John 5:1-18

# End of the Week

## Looking up:

Listen to "Open the Eyes of My Heart" and make it your prayer.

## Looking back:

1. Which day's devotion and passage of Scripture meant the most to you this week? Explain:

2. How has God made his presence known to you (in your prayers, study of the Scriptures, in quiet moments, busy times, and in conversations)?

3. How have you seen God's hand at work in your circumstances and in the lives of others this week?

4. How have you responded to temptation, and what help did you find at the most difficult moments?

5. What fruit of the Spirit (Galatians 5:22-23) would you like to see increase in your life? (Love, Joy, Peace, Patience, Kindness, Goodness, Gentleness, Faithfulness, Self-control) What difference would this make in your attitude, relationships, etc?

6. What opportunities has God given you to serve others, and how did you respond?

7. Did God provide an opportunity for you to share your faith with someone? What happened?

8. As you look to next week, what are some good choices you need to make?




In order to make those choices, Lord, I need you to. . . .

# MORE PRECIOUS THAN SILVER

Lord You are more precious than silver
Lord You are more costly than gold
Lord You are more beautiful than diamonds
And nothing I desire compares with You

Lord                         You are
   You are my Savior,   You are my Friend
More precious              than silver
   You're the beginning  And the end
Lord                         You are
   You are my Master,   Precious Lord
More costly                than gold
   You are my strength  Forevermore
Lord                         You are
   You are my Father    You are my King
More beautiful             than diamonds
   You're everything     That I need
And nothing I desire compares to you
Nothing I desire compares to You
Nothing compares to You . . . Nothing compares to You . . .

# Lifesaver

> "I tell you the truth, whoever hears my word and believes him who sent me has eternal life and will not be condemned; he has crossed over from death to life." (John 5:24)

Talk about promises!

Death is the most frightening thing people experience. We see life pass out of old people, and we wonder what happened to them. A friend dies a violent death, and we are shocked at the senselessness of it. In this conversation, Jesus gives us an incredible promise: for those who believe in him, he promises they will pass out of death to life. And this isn't an isolated promise. Jesus, Paul, and other writers make this same statement over and over again. (It's like they don't want us to miss it.)

We don't like to think about hell. It sounds awful—exactly because it is awful! People sometimes ask, "How can a loving God send anybody to hell?" The answer is: He doesn't. People make their own choices. It's like someone tossing a lifesaver to a drowning person and being told, "No thanks. I'll just keep struggling. Maybe I won't drown after all."

God has thrown the lifesaver. Each of us have it right in front of us, and the promise is that if we grab it, we will be rescued. And grabbing it doesn't just rescue us from hell. The package also includes being loved, accepted, and forgiven by the Creator of the Universe.

Cool!

 Lord Jesus, thank you that you made your promise of eternal life so clear. Thank you that you've rescued me from hell, and thank you that you've given me so much to live for.

☞ Listen to "More Precious Than Silver." Make it your prayer to God.

Read John 5:19-30

# Preventing Faith

> "How can you believe if you accept praise from one another, yet make no effort to obtain the praise that comes from the only God?" (John 5:44)

At another time and another place, Jesus told the crowd, "No one can serve two masters." That is the same message here. We can't have both people and God on the throne of our hearts. They don't fit. When we desire the approval of people more than the approval of God, it is a serious sin—a common one for sure, but deadly serious. In this passage in the Gospel of John, Jesus taught that actively seeking the praise (acceptance, honor, approval) of people actually prevents the development of our faith.

Approval is addictive. We get a little, and it feels good. After a while (minutes? seconds?), it wears off and we need it again. Soon we need a little more to satisfy us . . . and then a little more. Sounds like alcohol, doesn't it? Approval addiction can be just as damaging as a drug addiction. We can tell if we are caught up in approval addiction if we:

—compare our looks and achievements with others to see where we stack up,

—change our behavior to suit other people,

—think about others' reactions to us all day every day,

—put people down in order to lift ourselves up, or

—resent others who get praise.

Like any other addiction, the approval of men and women only feels good for a moment. It doesn't last. The incredible love and acceptance of God is strong and secure. It never changes. Enjoy it. Soak it in. It really satisfies.

 Jesus, your love means more to me than. . . .

 Write down evidences in your life of those five characteristics of approval addiction mentioned above. Confess them, accept God's forgiveness. Focus on his great love for you.

Read John 5:31-47

# Taking Tests

> When Jesus looked up and saw a great crowd coming toward him, he said to Philip, "Where shall we buy bread for these people to eat?" He asked him this only to test him, for he already had in mind what he was going to do. (John 6:5-6)

God puts us in situations all the time which test our faith. We come to a dead end; we face an impossible obstacle; we encounter unexpected opposition. We are faced with the question: "What are you going to do now?" This is essentially the question Jesus asked Philip (and I think Jesus had a smile on his face when he asked the question).

Philip had just witnessed several miracles of Jesus healing sick people. He had seen how Jesus taught about the kingdom of God. Now Jesus tested Philip to see if he had learned anything. God's goal in testing us is not to show us how dumb we are. It is to strengthen our faith. James wrote: "Consider it pure joy, my brothers, whenever you face trials of many kinds, because you know that the testing of your faith develops perseverance." If we have this perspective when we encounter each dead end, each obstacle, and each person who opposes us, we will respond, "This is great! God is strengthening my faith! I'm gonna grow through this!"

By the way, when Jesus tested Philip by asking him a question, Philip responded with a really dumb answer. Jesus didn't condemn him at all. He just did another miracle. Sometimes we pass the test. Sometimes we fail. But Jesus never fails.

 Jesus, I want to see the tests in my life as stepping stones for my faith. Thank you for these tests I am experiencing:

 Make a list of tests you have experienced over the past month. How would it have changed your response if you had believed these were designed to build your faith?

Read John 6:1-24

# Faith Alone

> Then they asked him, "What must we do to do the works God requires?"
>
> Jesus answered, "The work of God is this: to believe in the one he has sent." (John 6:28-29)

In virtually every other arena of our lives, performance is the key to success: we study to make good grades, we work hard to earn some money, we train to be good athletes, and we learn social skills to relate well to others. So it is only natural for people to ask, "What performance does God require of me?"

But the kingdom of God is different. It is based on faith, not performance. It is a gift; it can't be earned. As Christians, we sometimes slip back into that kind of thinking. We believe we became Christians by grace, but somehow our standing with God is now reduced to a checklist of things we do and don't do. When we slip into that thinking, we become self-righteous Pharisees (ouch!) who do the right things but miss the love and joy of life.

Jesus told them, "Don't worry about the 478,847 things other people say you have to do to please God. There's only one thing that counts: faith in me." If we have that faith, we will be tuned in to God's Spirit, our hearts will change, and we will want to please the One who loves us so much. At that point, we will want to fulfill all the commands found in the Scriptures—not because we are afraid not to, but because we want to honor God in any and every way we can. That's the power of true faith in Jesus.

 Lord Jesus, strip away all my misunderstandings of what it means to follow you so that my faith is strong and pure.

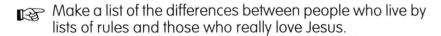 Make a list of the differences between people who live by lists of rules and those who really love Jesus.

Read John 6:25-59

> From this time many of his disciples turned back and no longer followed him.
> "You do not want to leave too, do you?" Jesus asked the Twelve.
> Simon Peter answered him, "Lord, to whom shall we go? You have the words of eternal life." (John 6:67-69)

The gospel of Jesus Christ is wonderfully attractive. He offers forgiveness, love, and meaning beyond anyone or anything we can imagine. But the gospel is also very demanding. Jesus expects our wholehearted devotion . . . and he deserves it.

Jesus was popular. Great crowds came to hear him speak and to see him heal the sick. Popularity, however, wasn't Jesus' goal. He wanted people to have a "simple and pure devotion" to him. He still does.

Most of those in the crowd enjoyed being entertained, but when Jesus asked for commitment, they walked away. Jesus then turned to the Twelve and asked if they, too, would walk away. Peter saw the issue clearly: Nothing and no one else can give what Jesus gives. Yes, being his disciple is demanding and difficult sometimes, but it is the greatest adventure a person can ever experience. And the real encouragement is that Jesus not only gives us truth and hope and direction. He gives us himself. No matter what he demands of us, he promises to always be as close as our breath.

 Lord Jesus, none of the other things in life that promise excitement and fulfillment can compare with knowing and following you. I am committed to you because. . . .

 Make a list of the things that promise to fulfill but ultimately are empty. (You might use categories of possessions, prestige, and people.)

Read John 6:60-71

# YOU ARE MY TREASURE

Faithful Lord fill my cup with Your grace and love,
Your grace and love
The pleasures that this world's sure of will never be enough,
can never be enough

'Cause I'm created for You alone
Bought with a price I'm not my own
Seated in the heavenlies
There's no place I'd rather be
than with You forever, Lord
You are my treasure

Than with You forever, Lord
Than with You forever, Lord
You are my treasure
You are my treasure
You are my treasure

You are my treasure

# End of the Week

## Looking up:
Listen to "You Are My Treasure." Pray it to the Lord.

## Looking back:
1. Which day's devotion and passage of Scripture meant the most to you this week? Explain:

2. How has God made his presence known to you (in your prayers, study of the Scriptures, in quiet moments, busy times, and in conversations)?

3. How have you seen God's hand at work in your circumstances and in the lives of others this week?

4. How have you responded to temptation, and what help did you find at the most difficult moments?

5. What fruit of the Spirit (Galatians 5:22-23) would you like to see increase in your life? (Love, Joy, Peace, Patience, Kindness, Goodness, Gentleness, Faithfulness, Self-control) What difference would this make in your attitude, relationships, etc?

6. What opportunities has God given you to serve others, and how did you respond?

7. Did God provide an opportunity for you to share your faith with someone? What happened?

8. As you look to next week, what are some good choices you need to make?

In order to make those choices, Lord, I need you to. . . .

# THE HAPPY SONG

I could sing unending songs of
how You saved my soul
I could dance a thousand miles
because of Your great love

My heart is bursting, Lord,
To tell of all You've done
Of how You changed my life and wiped away the past
I want to shout it out, from every rooftop sing
For now I know that God is for me not against me

I could sing unending songs of
how You saved my soul
I could dance a thousand miles
because of Your great love

# Day 1     Learning to Wait

> Therefore Jesus told them, "The right time for me has not yet come. . . ." (John 7:6)

We live in an instant society: microwave ovens, fast Internet access, drive-thru windows, remote controls. We hate to wait. The kingdom of God, however, doesn't operate on a 56K modem at 500mhz. Waiting is an important part of the process of spiritual growth.

God delays answers to prayer for many different reasons. Here are a few:

—He wants us to pray more earnestly.

—He uses this time to purify our motives.

—He uses this process to change our desires and our direction.

—He wants us to pursue him more than the answer to our prayer.

—He is working in other people's lives and in other circumstances, and the blessing will be multiplied when he brings it all together.

—He is testing us to see if we will stay strong in our faith as we wait.

Waiting is not just passing time. When the word "wait" is used in the Scriptures, it means to expect God to come through. David wrote:

> I am still confident of this:
> I will see the goodness of the Lord
> in the land of the living.
> Wait for the Lord;
> be strong and take heart
> and wait for the Lord. (Psalm 27:13-14)

 Lord, thank you for slowing me down so I can focus on you. As I wait for you, I expect you to. . . .

☞ What are you waiting for (expecting) God to do in your life today?

Read John 7:1-24

# The Real Thing

> Jesus stood and said in a loud voice, "If anyone is thirsty, let him come to me and drink. Whoever believes in me, as the Scripture has said, streams of living water will flow from within him." (John 7:37-38)

All of us are spiritually thirsty. It's a natural and normal part of the human condition. Every culture in all of history has tried in some way to quench that thirst. In our culture, people try to fill up their spiritual tanks and find meaning from all kinds of things: pleasure, approval, academics, sports, horoscopes, and many other sources.

But these things are like drinking milk when you are hot and thirsty. It only makes you more thirsty.

Jesus was in a huge crowd of people who were seeking God. He yelled to get their attention, and then he told them what they all needed to hear: "Take a big drink of me. I'll satisfy you. And even more than that, I'll flow through you and use you to satisfy lots of other people." I can almost hear the people listening say, "Man, it doesn't get any better than this!"

All these other things promise to satisfy, but they can't. They simply can't. Only Christ can quench our spiritual thirst, and pursuing him is the most important purpose of our lives. Paul wrote to the Philippians: "I consider everything I have accomplished and own to be rubbish compared to the surpassing greatness of knowing Christ." (paraphrased)

Nothing else compares. He's the real thing.

 Lord Jesus, I want to drink of you because. . . .

 Listen to "The Happy Song."

Read John 7:25-53

# Day 3 Stonethrowers or Forgivers?

> The teachers of the law and the Pharisees brought in a woman caught in adultery. They made her stand before the group and said to Jesus, "Teacher, this woman was caught in the act of adultery. In the Law Moses commanded us to stone such women. Now what do you say?" (John 8:3-5)

Sin is serious business. Our sin was the reason Jesus had to die. We should never take it lightly and say, "Oh, it doesn't matter. Nobody really cares."

The lawyers and the Pharisees knew that this woman's sin demanded judgment. They failed to realize, however, that true forgiveness doesn't gloss over the gravity of sin. Genuine forgiveness embraces all the ugliness and horror of sin, and still chooses not to take revenge.

Philip Yancey wrote an article about forgiveness several years ago titled "The Unnatural Act." He said that everything in us cries out for justice—for revenge—when someone offends us. Like the lawyers and the Pharisees, we want to throw stones at the one who sinned. Those stones take the form of gossip, angry stares, withdrawal, yelling, cussing, or other forms of punishment.

Jesus had a better way.

We can forgive others only to the degree we have experienced Christ's forgiveness ourselves. Paul wrote: "Be kind to one another, tenderhearted, forgiving one another just as God in Christ has forgiven you." (Eph. 4:32) When someone hurts you, don't throw a stone. Think about the incredible forgiveness you have received from Christ, and make the hard choice to forgive that other person.

 Jesus, I want to be so overwhelmed with your forgiveness of my sins that I. . . .

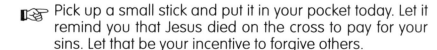 Pick up a small stick and put it in your pocket today. Let it remind you that Jesus died on the cross to pay for your sins. Let that be your incentive to forgive others.

Read John 8:1-11

# All Day Every Day

"The one who sent me is with me; he has not left me alone, for I always do what pleases him." (John 8:29)

Some of us do something really strange: we compartmentalize our lives into what is sacred (youth group, retreats, prayer meetings, church) and secular (everything else). When we are in the "sacred" activities, we are aware of God's presence and his purposes, but as soon as we walk out the door, we think and act as if God doesn't exist. Somehow we think that God cares about worship, but not about geometry; about prayer, but not what music we listen to; about the truth of the Scriptures, but not how we relate to our friends at school.

Every single aspect of our lives is a gift from God and is to be lived to the fullest for his honor. We need his direction just as much on Tuesday afternoon in Spanish class as we do on Sunday morning in Bible study.

Jesus certainly didn't compartmentalize his life. He lived every moment aware of the Father's purposes for him. When he taught the truth to the crowds of disciples, he did it to please the Father. And when he walked along the roads listening to his friends tell jokes, he pleased the Father by listening and valuing those people. His one consuming desire all day every day was: I want to please the Father in every thought, every conversation, and every action.

We can please the Father all day every day, too.

 Father, you can give me direction, peace, and a sense of your presence at every moment of every day.

 Put a small rock in your pocket today. Every time you feel it, remember that God is with you, and you can please him at that very moment.

Read John 8:12-41

# Day 5     Lethal Whispers

> "You belong to your father, the devil, and you want to carry out your father's desire. He was a murderer from the beginning, not holding to the truth, for there is no truth in him. When he lies, he speaks his native language, for he is a liar and the father of lies." (John 8:44)

Make no mistake: the devil is very real, and he hates your guts. One of his favorite ways to hurt us is to tell us lies. He whispers in our ears:
—"You're no good."
—"You can't ever do enough to make up for what you've done."
—"Nobody cares about you."
—"How could you have done something so stupid?"
—"You're not even a Christian."

The problem is that he uses our own voices when he tells us those things, so we usually don't even identify those thoughts as lies from the pit of hell—which they are. Paul instructs us to "take every thought captive to the obedience of Christ." We do that by holding each thought up to the light of the truth of God: Does it line up with Scripture? Is it full of God's grace? Does it build up or tear down? These questions quickly reveal the source of these messages. When God convicts us of sin, it is always with the promise of forgiveness and the hope of change. When Satan condemns us for our sins, his desire is to crush us. Don't get them confused!

If you wonder if the messages in your mind are from Satan, talk to your youth pastor or a trusted, mature Christian friend. You'll soon find out the truth. Then cling to the truth of your forgiveness, acceptance, and love in Christ. That's the message to let your mind dwell on.

 Lord, thank you for showing me which thoughts are from you and which are from the devil. The messages I want to focus on are. . . .

☞ What messages has Satan consistently used to confuse and discourage you?

Read John 8:42-59

# End of the Week

<u>Looking up:</u>
Listen to "The Happy Song." Make it a prayer.

<u>Looking back:</u>
1. Which day's devotion and passage of Scripture meant the most to you this week? Explain:

2. How has God made his presence known to you (in your prayers, study of the Scriptures, in quiet moments, busy times, and in conversations)?

3. How have you seen God's hand at work in your circumstances and in the lives of others this week?

4. How have you responded to temptation, and what help did you find at the most difficult moments?

5. What fruit of the Spirit (Galatians 5:22-23) would you like to see increase in your life? (Love, Joy, Peace, Patience, Kindness, Goodness, Gentleness, Faithfulness, Self-control) What difference would this make in your attitude, relationships, etc?

6. What opportunities has God given you to serve others, and how did you respond?

7. Did God provide an opportunity for you to share your faith with someone? What happened?

8. As you look to next week, what are some good choices you need to make?

In order to make those choices, Lord, I need you to. . . .

# I WILL ARISE

I will arise and sing of the
mercy that You give
I will arise and sing again and again

You've broken all the chains and
Your love is within me
I will arise and sing
'Cause I know that You live

And I will arise, I will arise.
I will arise and sing to You my King
for You are the risen Lamb

And I will arise, I will arise
I will arise to You
You are faithful and true
And You are the great I AM
I will arise

# What Now?

> As he went along, he saw a man blind from birth. His disciples asked him, "Rabbi, who sinned, this man or his parents, that he was born blind?" (John 9:1-2)

We have lots of questions. We want answers. Why was this person killed in the wreck and that person spared? Why was that person chosen for an award and another person overlooked? Why did this person get sick? Why did that person have to move away?

Jesus had an answer to his disciples. He said, in effect: "You're asking the wrong question." The real issue is: how does God want to use this situation so that "the work of God can be displayed."

There are many things we don't understand, and there will always be things that we just don't get. The question we need to ask is not "Why?" but "What now?" The "Why?" questions drive us crazy. We demand to find an answer, but we the more we dig, the more confused we become. Sooner or later (preferably sooner), we need to do what Jesus suggested: embrace the mysterious sovereignty of God and look for what he wants to accomplish through the sickness, death, or difficulty. When we trust God in the middle of our struggles and confusion, he is able to reveal his wisdom, strength, love, and grace in us and through us.

God doesn't cause tragedies, but he wants to use them to strengthen and deepen us.

 Lord, I have asked "Why?" about _____. Now I want to ask "What now?" Please give me your wisdom and peace about this.

 What has happened in your family or in your school in the past few months that people have asked, "Why, God?" How might God want to display his love and grace in these situations?

Read John 9:1-12

# Touched

He replied, ". . . One thing I know. I was blind but now I see!" (John 9:25)

The blind man who received his sight had gone to the synagogue every week for many years. He probably heard lots of good teaching and solid theology. There's nothing in the world wrong with right teaching, but it is empty apart from genuine experience.

The moment that Jesus touched his life, everything changed. The theology didn't become meaningless. No, it became rich and real. Now the teaching about the love and power of God jumped off the pages (or the scrolls) and became flesh and blood. Now the passages about the presence of God found expression in a man named Jesus who had spit on the ground, made some clay, and rubbed it on his eyes.

This man's experience gave him joy, and it also gave him strength. He was criticized and condemned by religious leaders who threatened to kick him out of the synagogue if he continued to give Jesus credit for the miracle. The man didn't hesitate. The fact that he could now see convinced him that Jesus was the Messiah. He almost blurted out, "Well, hey, look at me! I was blind and now I can see!"

Experience apart from truth is dangerous and misleading, but experience based on truth gives courage, hope, and joy. Have you let Jesus touch your life? What are you waiting for?

 Jesus, touch my life. Make yourself real to me again. . . .

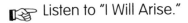 Listen to "I Will Arise."

Read John 9:13-34

# Day 3     Upside Down

> Jesus said, "For judgment I have come into this world, so that the blind will see and those who see will become blind." (John 9:39)

This is one of those statements of Jesus that we read, then we scratch our heads and say something really profound like, "Huh? What in the world was he talking about?"

Jesus had just met the man who had received his sight. Jesus knew the man had been thrown out of the synagogue by the jealous religious leaders because the man gave credit to Jesus for healing him. Jesus' statement means that he is shaking up the establishment. He turns the world upside down. Blind people miraculously gain their sight because they believe in him, but religious leaders who think they are so wise and perceptive are shown to be spiritually blind when they refuse to believe the truth. Their pride is blindness, and their cynicism keeps them in the dark.

I believe Jesus' statement is both an invitation and a warning. It is an invitation for us to be honest about our hurts, stupidity, and sins so that we turn to the one who can make us whole. And it is a warning to those of us who have been in the church for a while (yes, even young people) not to become so comfortable and full of pride that we stop sensing our great need for Christ.

Respond to the invitation and experience his healing presence.

Wake up to the warning and stay fresh in your relationship with Jesus.

 Lord Jesus, I am well aware of my need for you. . . .

☞ Take a few minutes to do an inventory on your heart. In what ways are you aware of your need for God to work in and through you, and in what ways are you too cocky and confident in yourself?

Read John 9:35-41

# Destructive Counterfeits

"The thief comes only to steal and kill and destroy; I have come that they may have life, and have it to the full."
(John 10:10)

Sometimes I walk down a crowded sidewalk and wonder who the people are I am walking past. What are their lives like? What makes them happy? What hurts do they hide? That guy looks like he's rich. That girl looks sad. I wonder which of these people (not if any of these people) have committed crimes in the past week or two!

Most thieves look like most other people we pass on the street. We can't identify them until we see the results of their crimes. In the same way, the thief Jesus talked about, Satan, disguises his work very carefully so we can't tell what he is doing is evil. One of his most effective methods of stealing life from us is to attract us with counterfeit goals. He tries to make us believe that if we can just have enough success, enough good times, or enough people like us, then our lives will be rich and full. And plenty of people believe it! Even Christians.

Satan sneaks around filling our minds with messages in advertisements, movies, popular songs, and in conversations with friends. We believe that we have to have a faster car, flashier clothes, more money, acceptance by those friends, sex with that person, or a zillion other things to be really happy. But look at the people who pursue those things. Are they really happy? I don't think so. The pursuit of those things steals our contentment, kills our good motives, and destroys our relationships.

But Jesus offers us the great adventure of our lives, the thrill of knowing him and watching him use us to change the world around us.

Man, what a difference!

 Lord Jesus, show me the counterfeits in my life so that I can repent and put you and your purposes first again.

 Take some time alone to let God speak to you about any counterfeits in your life.

Read John 10:1-21

# Being Sure

> "My sheep listen to my voice; I know them, and they fol-
> low me. I give them eternal life, and they shall never perish;
> no one can snatch them out of my hand. My Father, who has
> given them to me, is greater than all; no one can snatch them
> out of my Father's hand. I and the Father are one."
> (John 10:27-30)

A survey of people who attend church regularly showed that half of them were not sure that they would go to heaven if they died that day. I assume the same percentage applies to young people. And it makes me sad.

It is very difficult to respond to the Father's voice if we aren't sure we're a part of the family. Young people already deal with some of the toughest questions in life, like: Where do I fit in? and Does anybody care about me? Some of us see God as cruel or distant. We need God to be an anchor in the storm, not another wave.

In this passage, Jesus gives us a promise that if we have trusted in him, he has us securely in his strong, loving hand. And to make his point even more, he says that the Father has us in his hand, too. You can't get any more secure than that!

God doesn't want us to wonder if he loves us. He wants us to be sure. The new birth occurs when we acknowledge our sinfulness to God and accept Christ's death on the cross as the payment for our sins. At that moment, amazing things happen to us: we are delivered from the kingdom of Satan into the kingdom of God; all our sins are forgiven; we receive eternal life; and we are accepted into the family of God.

And on top of that, we have the promise of Jesus that he has us right where we belong: in his hands.

 Jesus, thank you for holding me. . . .

 Take some time to be alone and quiet. Imagine yourself being held in Jesus hands. How does that make you feel about him? . . . about yourself?

Read John 10:22-42

# End of the Week

## Looking up:
Listen to "I Will Arise" and pray it to the Lord.

## Looking back:
1. Which day's devotion and passage of Scripture meant the most to you this week? Explain:

2. How has God made his presence known to you (in your prayers, study of the Scriptures, in quiet moments, busy times, and in conversations)?

3. How have you seen God's hand at work in your circumstances and in the lives of others this week?

4. How have you responded to temptation, and what help did you find at the most difficult moments?

5. What fruit of the Spirit (Galatians 5:22-23) would you like to see increase in your life? (Love, Joy, Peace, Patience, Kindness, Goodness, Gentleness, Faithfulness, Self-control) What difference would this make in your attitude, relationships, etc?

6. What opportunities has God given you to serve others, and how did you respond?

7. Did God provide an opportunity for you to share your faith with someone? What happened?

8. As you look to next week, what are some good choices you need to make?

In order to make those choices, Lord, I need you to. . . .

# BLESSED BE THE NAME

Blessed be the name of the Lord
Blessed be the name of the Lord
Blessed be the name of the Lord Most High

The name of the Lord is a strong tower
The righteous run in and they are saved
The name of the Lord is a strong tower
The righteous run in and they are saved

Holy is the name of the Lord . . .

Jesus is the name of the Lord . . .

Blessed be the name of the Lord
Blessed be the name of the Lord
Blessed by the name of the Lord Most High

Jesus is the name of the Lord
Jesus is the name of the Lord
Jesus is the name of the Lord
Holy is the name of the Lord
Blessed is the name of the Lord Most High

# A Real Man

> Jesus wept. (John 11:35)

Sometimes I sing in churches which have stained glass windows. Many of them show Jesus looking vaguely sad . . . or kind of smiling. When you look at these images week after week, it's easy to think that Jesus is just as lifeless and boring as that glass!

He isn't.

Sure, Jesus is the Creator of the Universe, the Alpha and the Omega, the King of kings and Lord of lords, but he was—and is—a person who expressed the full range of emotion. At the tomb of his friend Lazarus, he was overcome with sadness—and he cried. When he saw the Temple being used as a shop for merchants to make money, he was angry and ran them out. When he held children in his arms, he stroked their hair and smiled. And I can imagine Jesus walking down the road or sitting around a campfire with his disciples and having some great laughs together. After all, he called them his friends, and that's what friends do together.

How do you envision Jesus back then . . . and today? Take him out of the stained glass and imagine him as flesh and blood: smiling, laughing, grimacing, and crying. He is certainly not some impersonal "Force." His disciples loved him because they felt his love. They respected and obeyed him because they saw the powerful blend of his strength and compassion. He's the same today. Right now. With me. And with you.

 Lord Jesus, you aren't stained glass or bronze or plaster. You are real, and you call me your friend. Help me feel your smile. . . .

 Write down your answers to these questions: What things about your life (in your heart, in your family, in your school, etc.) make Jesus smile? . . . laugh? . . . angry? . . . cry?

Read John 11:1-37

# Taking Off the Grave Clothes

When he had said this, Jesus called in a loud voice, "Lazarus, come out!" The dead man came out, his hands and his feet wrapped with strips of linen, and a cloth around his face.

Jesus said to them, "Take off the grave clothes and let him go." (John 11:43-44)

Jesus had performed a miracle: he had brought a dead man back to life! But Lazarus stood there wrapped in linen strips like a mummy. He couldn't move! What was Jesus' solution? He told the people around him to help him by taking the linen off so he could experience his freedom.

That is a beautiful picture of what needs to happen when someone receives Christ. At that moment, a dead person miraculously is brought to life. But quite often, that person is still wrapped up by attitudes, behaviors, and relationships from the past. He needs someone—you and me—to help get those things off so he can be free to follow Christ. Let me give you some examples:

—For a person who has been involved in drugs, we can take him to a doctor or a counselor to get treatment.

—For a someone who has been hanging out with a rough crowd, we can invite her to spend time with us—a lot of time with us.

—For a person who has a foul mouth, we can model good communication and maybe, just maybe, point out how that language displeases God.

—For someone who has been immobilized by fear, we can give plenty of encouragement and hope.

All of us have "grave clothes" when we become Christians. Be one of those who lovingly serves to take those off others so they can be truly free.

 Lord, as I read this, I thought of _____. Give me wisdom about how I can help take the grave clothes off that person.

 What were your grave clothes when you became a Christian?

Read John 11:38-57

# Day 3     Lavish Love

> Then Mary took about a pint of pure nard, an expensive perfume; she poured it on Jesus' feet and wiped his feet with her hair. And the house was filled with the fragrance of the perfume. (John 12:3)

Mary and her sister Martha already loved Jesus, but when Jesus raised their brother Lazarus from the dead, Mary couldn't contain her appreciation! She spent a ton of money on some perfume and then poured the whole bottle out on Jesus' feet. She didn't stop there. She bent down and wiped his feet with her hair.

I'm afraid of getting so busy that I miss out on seeing God at work all around me. And when I don't see his hand at work, my heart can grow cold. But if I take the time to notice God working in my life and in the lives of those around me, I am much more like Mary—absolutely overcome with appreciation and affection for Jesus! She poured out lavish love for him simply as a response to his lavish love for her and her brother.

But keep reading. One of the disciples gave Mary some major flak for being so extravagant in her love. When you and I express unbounded love for Jesus, there will probably be those (even those in our youth groups) who snicker or sneer at us. Here's some advice: Blow 'em off. Don't even think about them. Keep your eyes focused on the one who loves you and is powerfully at work all around you.

Don't try to manufacture this kind of love for Jesus. It doesn't work that way. Our love for him is always a response to feeling, seeing, and knowing his great love for us. Then . . . be lavish in your love for him.

 Jesus, open my eyes to see your loving hand at work around me today.

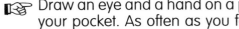 Draw an eye and a hand on a piece of paper and put it in your pocket. As often as you feel it today, look for God's hand at work around you.

Read John 12:1-19

> "But I, when I am lifted up from the earth, will draw all men to myself." (John 12:32)

When Jesus' cross was lifted and slammed into its hole on the hill outside Jerusalem, people from all around could see the spectacle. Most of them saw it as a sign of horror and shame, but a few, like the Roman soldier at Jesus' feet, saw and believed.

Today, people from all around still see the spectacle. There are churches in every community and missionaries in every foreign country. The good news of Christ's forgiveness can be found in Bibles in every hotel room, on every television, and on quite a few highway overpasses! God is calling all men to himself.

As I pray for lost people, I ask God to bring his truth and grace into their lives. Time after time, I hear that God sent this Christian or caused that experience, this Bible or that Christian celebrity's message into that person's life. I'm convinced that Jesus is actively calling to people all around us, "Hey, look at me! I love you so much that I died for you."

Sometimes we think evangelism is mostly up to us. It's not. God is the one who draws people to himself. And it is our incredible privilege to have a part in that: by praying, by speaking, by bringing, and by living and loving those people.

I just hope they listen.

 Jesus, you are at work today to draw people to yourself. Thank you for letting me be a part of that process by. . . .

☞ Think of one lost person you know. Pray for God to bring people and circumstances into that person's life to make them hungry for Christ. And then watch.

Read John 12:20-50

# Day 5     The Full Extent

> It was just before the Passover Feast. Jesus knew that the time had come for him to leave this world and go to the Father. Having loved his own who were in the world, he now showed them the full extent of his love. (John 13:1)

Everything up to this point had been the previews. The miracles, the talks to the crowds, the walks and the campfires. . . . Jesus had shown his love to all kinds of people in all kinds of ways. But now it was time for the feature presentation. He was going to show them "the full extent of his love."

He was going to die to pay for their sins. A horrible, excruciating, shameful death.

Jesus didn't die suddenly in car wreck. A doctor didn't walk in and say, "I'm sorry. You have cancer, and you have only two weeks to live." Nothing that happened to Jesus in those last days was a surprise. He knew exactly what was coming. Crucifixion was one of the most painful types of torture ever invented by evil men. . . .

—Lashed by a whip which had bits of glass and bone to tear the flesh on his back.

—Muscle and tendons ripped by nails and pulled by his own weight.

—Terrible thirst, shooting pangs, slow suffocation.

—But far more painful than these was that Jesus was separated from the Father so his wrath could be poured out on the sins—yours and mine—Jesus carried.

He could have stepped down at any time. He could have called 10,000 angels to wipe out the entire human race and end his suffering. But he didn't. The "full extent of his love" was shown when he willingly suffered the agony of the cross. For you. And for me.

 Lord Jesus, you didn't have to die for me, but you did it willingly. Thank you. . . .

 Listen to "Blessed Be the Name."

Read John 13:1-11

# End of the Week

## Looking up:
Listen to " Blessed Be the Name." Make it a prayer.

## Looking back:
1. Which day's devotion and passage of Scripture meant the most to you this week? Explain:

2. How has God made his presence known to you (in your prayers, study of the Scriptures, in quiet moments, busy times, and in conversations)?

3. How have you seen God's hand at work in your circumstances and in the lives of others this week?

4. How have you responded to temptation, and what help did you find at the most difficult moments?

5. What fruit of the Spirit (Galatians 5:22-23) would you like to see increase in your life? (Love, Joy, Peace, Patience, Kindness, Goodness, Gentleness, Faithfulness, Self-control) What difference would this make in your attitude, relationships, etc?

6. What opportunities has God given you to serve others, and how did you respond?

7. Did God provide an opportunity for you to share your faith with someone? What happened?

8. As you look to next week, what are some good choices you need to make?




In order to make those choices, Lord, I need you to. . . .

# IN THE SECRET

In the secret, in the quiet place
In the stillness You are there
In the secret, in the quiet hour I wait
Only for You
'Cause I want to know You more

I want to know You
I want to hear Your voice
I want to know You more
I want to touch You
I want to see Your face
I want to know You more

I'm reaching for the highest goal
That I might receive the prize
Pressing onward, pushing every hinderance aside
Out of my way
Because I want to know You more

# Secret Service

> "Now that I, your Lord and Teacher, have washed your feet, you also should wash one another's feet. I have set you an example that you should do as I have done for you." (John 13:14-15)

Jesus was a fantastic teacher. He was an even better servant. He spoke marvelous truth in the Sermon on the Mount and in a hundred other speeches, but when he wanted to teach about being a servant, the King of kings became like the lowest slave. He put on an apron and washed the feet of each of his disciples—even Judas.

One of the best ways to tell if a person is a true disciple of Jesus is to gauge their behavior on a servant-o-meter. How often does that person expect others to do the grunt work like buying the donuts, welcoming new people, and cleaning up. The real test of a servant is that he does these things without calling attention to himself. If he says by words or actions, "Look at me! I'm serving now!", a true servant's heart is missing.

Another test of a servant is that he serves those he doesn't really like. Jesus washed Judas' feet on the night Judas was going to betray him for 30 silver coins. Do you have people in your life who you'd rather avoid? Of course, you do. Everybody does. Jesus wants us to serve them, too.

Be a "secret service servant." Do things for other people without being asked and without calling attention to your actions. And do something kind for somebody you don't like—your little brother, maybe. That's what Jesus did. You can, too.

 Lord, you don't ask me to do anything you didn't do for other people. Help me serve others by. . . .

 Be a "secret service servant" today. Make it a point to pitch in and help several people without being asked. (And help them get up when they faint!)

Read John 13:12-17

# Who Are You?

> One of them, the disciple whom Jesus loved, was reclining next to him. (John 13:23)

Who are you? How do you identify yourself? When you meet someone new, what do you say about yourself? In John's gospel, he identified himself as "the disciple whom Jesus loved." Was he the only one Jesus loved? Of course not. He loved them, and he loves you and me just as much as he loved them.

Sometimes theologians describe John as being a bit, well, not a manly man because he talked so much about love. That's ridiculous! John and his brother James were called the "sons of thunder." What kind of guys do you think would be called "sons of thunder"? Yeah, tough guys. Take-no-prisoners kind of men. But the kindness, tenderness, and gentleness of Jesus penetrated that tough exterior and melted John's heart. That love was so overwhelming that for the rest of his life, he thought of himself primarily as being "the disciple whom Jesus loved."

What difference would that make to you and me? Jesus loves us just as much as he loved John. If we grasp the depth of that kindness, it will melt our hearts, too. And it will give us courage. John was faithful to Jesus to the end. Legend tells us that he was boiled in oil when he refused to renounce Christ. Man, that took guts! If you and I are overwhelmed with the love of Jesus, we will have enough courage to live for him all day every day.

His love is worth it.

 Jesus, I want to be so convinced of your great love that I think of myself as "the disciple whom Jesus loves," just like John.

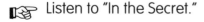 Listen to "In the Secret."

Read John 13:18-30

# Day 3  The Whole World Notices

> "A new command I give you; Love one another. As I have loved you, so you must love one another. By this all men will know that you are my disciples, if you love one another." (John 13:34-35)

How did Jesus love people? He didn't make fun of them when they asked stupid questions. He patiently waited for them to understand—and waited and waited. He reached out to them when it was inconvenient. He touched lepers whose flesh was putrid. He picked up little children who were considered pests by others.

He let himself be killed to pay for their sins. That's a lot of love.

The Bible distinguishes between brotherly phileo love and God's agape love. One is nice; the other is revolutionary. Brotherly love is when we enjoy hanging out with people who like us. That, Jesus said, is no big deal: "Even sinners love those who love them." But God's love makes headlines. When we forgive someone who has betrayed us and we refuse to take revenge, that's agape. When we reach out quietly to help people who can't repay us, that's the work of God in our hearts. When we take time to listen patiently and attentively to a boring person, that's the real thing, too.

Theology is important, especially when it is under attack like it is today, but theology alone doesn't change lives. Love does. Agape is theology in action. It is truth with feet; it is God using our hands and our voices to communicate his love to other people.

And when we practice that kind of love, the whole world notices. The problem is that we settle for brotherly love far too often. Nobody notices that.

 Jesus, fill me with your love, and open my eyes to see those around me who are in need of being loved.

☞ Show agape love today to one person: an outcast, a bore, an ugly person, or one of your parents.

Read John 13:31-38

# Sit Back, Get Stomped

"Do not let your hearts be troubled. Trust in God; trust also in me." (John 14:1)

When we "let" something happen, we sit back and watch it occur. In this passage, Jesus says that we have to be careful not to let our hearts get bent out of shape. If we sit back and just watch life go by, that's exactly what will happen. The criticisms, doubts, and heartaches we all experience will slowly (or not so slowly) overwhelm us, and we give up.

In his letter to the Ephesians, Paul tells them to "take up the shield of faith" as a part of the armor of God, "with which you extinguish all the flaming arrows of the evil one." A shield is held by the warrior's hand. It can be turned to the right or the left to deflect the arrows. If the warrior just "lets" the shield hang at his side, he'll get shafted!

Jesus said, "Trust God." That's what Paul said, too. Trust is active. It is like a muscle that is strengthened when we use it, and it becomes weak when we just let it hang. Our faith in Christ requires constant exercise for it to grow strong. That faith is demonstrated in the face of opportunities or obstacles, times when we are advancing the kingdom or times we are defending ourselves or others from attack.

Paul realized we are in a war. No soldier can be safe and effective by letting the enemy shoot at him without holding up his shield. We can't be passive in our spiritual fight either. Listen to our commander, obey his orders, trust that his resources of truth and grace are exactly what we need to win.

 Jesus, I need to take up my shield of faith and be strong in order to face. . . .

 What are some negative things that happen when we are spiritually passive?

Read John 14:1-4

# Day 5     Greater Things?

> "I tell you the truth, anyone who has faith in me will do what I have been doing. He will do even greater things than these, because I am going to the Father." (John 14:12)

This is one of those statements that it's easy to respond, "You gotta be kidding!" But the disciples experienced the fulfillment of this promise. They had watched Jesus heal the sick, cast out demons, and preach the gospel, then one day Jesus turned to them and said, "OK, guys, pair up. You are going out to do what you've seen me do. Don't worry. The power that has worked through me will be working through you. Have a great time now. Send me a postcard." They went out, and sure enough, God used them to do all the things they had seen Jesus do!

But what about the next part of this promise? Greater things? Come on. Who can do greater things than Jesus? I believe that Jesus was talking about quantity, not quality. Because his Spirit would reside in hundreds, then thousands, and then millions of believers, we could take the healing gospel of Christ to people all over the world—much farther than the area Jesus traveled.

Pretty exciting stuff, huh? Do you see the qualifier in this promise? Jesus said "anyone who has faith in me." The disciples had their faith built because they spent lots of time with Jesus, watching, listening, talking, reflecting. Their faith didn't happen because they heard him once or ate with him on Tuesdays. Their faith was the product of years of intimate communication, seeing him love and watching him heal, listening to his laugh and marveling at his kindness.

And their faith grew.

Ours can too.

 Lord, I want to spend as much time aware of your presence as possible so that. . . .

☞ Listen to "Did You Feel the Mountains Tremble?" Is Jesus using you to do what he did . . . and even greater things? Why or why not?

Read John 14:5-14

# DID YOU FEEL THE MOUNTAINS TREMBLE?

Did you feel the mountains tremble
Did you hear the oceans roar
When the people rose to sing of
Jesus Christ the risen One

Did you feel the people tremble
Did you hear the singers roar
When the lost began to sing of
Jesus Christ the saving One

We can see that God You're moving
A mighty river through the nations
Young and old will turn to Jesus

Fling wide you heavenly gates
Prepare the way of the risen Lord

Open up the doors, let the music play
Let the streets resound with singing
Songs that bring Your hope
Songs that bring Your joy
Dancers who dance upon injustice

Do you feel the darkness tremble
When All the saints join in one song
All the streams flow as one river
To wash away our brokenness

We can see that God You're moving
A time of jubilee is coming
Young and old return to Jesus

Fling wide you heavenly gates
Prepare the way of the risen Lord

Did you feel the mountains tremble
Did you hear the oceans roar
When the people rose to sing of
Jesus Christ the risen One

Martin Smith © Curious? Music UK Admin. by Birdwing Music in US &
Canada, ASCAP c/o EMI Christian Music Publishing. All rights reserved.
Used by permission. Conclusion of song appears on this page.

# End of the Week

## Looking up:
Listen to "Did You Feel the Mountains Tremble?" Make it your prayer.

## Looking back:
1. Which day's devotion and passage of Scripture meant the most to you this week? Explain:

2. How has God made his presence known to you (in your prayers, study of the Scriptures, in quiet moments, busy times, and in conversations)?

3. How have you seen God's hand at work in your circumstances and in the lives of others this week?

4. How have you responded to temptation, and what help did you find at the most difficult moments?

5. What fruit of the Spirit (Galatians 5:22-23) would you like to see increase in your life? (Love, Joy, Peace, Patience, Kindness, Goodness, Gentleness, Faithfulness, Self-control) What difference would this make in your attitude, relationships, etc?

6. What opportunities has God given you to serve others, and how did you respond?

7. Did God provide an opportunity for you to share your faith with someone? What happened?

8. As you look to next week, what are some good choices you need to make?

In order to make those choices, Lord, I need you to. . . .

# BE GLORIFIED

Your love has captured me
Your grace has set me free
You're life, the air I breathe
Be glorified in me

You set my feet to dancing
You set my heart on fire
In the presence of a thousand kings
You are my one desire
I stand before You now
With trembling hands lifted high

Lord be glorified

Be glorified in me
Be glorified in me
Be glorified in me
Be glorified in me

# Day 1 Fixing Your Motivation

"If you love me, you will obey what I command."
(John 14:15)

Seminary professor John Hannah says that the simplest and most profound definition of the Christian life is "obedience out of gratitude." I like that.

Many of us get all hung up on the obedience thing. We see it as a whip to keep us in line. The Christian life is shaped only by the 797,987 "don't's" and the 898,344 "do's," and we hope that God grades on a curve because we sure aren't doing all that great in class!

There are two very positive motivations for obedience: to escape pain and to show our love. When we sin (we could make a long list here, or we could just say that sin is anything that is against the will of God), we experience negative consequences. Maybe immediately; probably later. When we realize that much of our pain comes from not following God's path, it doesn't take a rocket scientist to wake up and make better decisions!

And the second motivation is to simply please the one who loves us so much. The more we grasp the great love of God, the more we want every word, thought, and action to make him smile. Paul said it this way: "For Christ's love compels us . . . that those who live should no longer live for themselves but for him who died for them and was raised again." (II Cor 5:14-15)

When we have even the slightest understanding of the grace of God, we obey because we want to, not because we have to.

Jesus, fill me with your love so that my "have to" is changed into a "want to."

What is one thing you know God wants you to do? How would being convinced of his love change your motivation to do it?

Read John 14:15-24

# A Different Peace

"Peace I leave with you; my peace I give you. I do not give it to you as the world gives. Do not let your hearts be troubled, and do not be afraid." (John 14:27)

Jesus' peace is very different from the peace the world offers. The world says that you can have freedom from hassles. If you have enough money, if you look great, if you have nice clothes and cars, and if you are popular, then hey, you've got it made! Most people (including a lot of Christians) buy this promise and pursue these things all day every day.

And they experience the very opposite of peace: fear, heartache, anxiety, and resentment.

The peace Jesus offers is experienced in the middle of hassles, not in the absence of them. No matter what happens, we can be absolutely sure that he is in control, he understands, he cares, and he is right here with us.

David learned a lot about experiencing the peace of God. In one of his most popular psalms, he described the peace he felt even when he was in danger. He wrote:

> Even though I walk through
> the valley of the shadow of death,
> I will fear no evil,
> for you are with me:
> your rod and your staff,
> they comfort me. (Psalm 23:4)

When you and I feel stressed, bummed, or attacked, we need to remember that the solution is not always the escape from our problems; quite often it is to experience God's presence in the middle of our problems. In him we find peace, comfort, and direction.

 Lord Jesus, today I need to sense your presence to give me peace because. . . .

 Put a mark on the back of your hand. Every time you look at it today, remember that Jesus is with you, and he gives you peace.

Read John 14:25-31

# Day 3 The Purpose of Pruning

> "I am the true vine, and my Father is the gardener. He cuts off every branch in me that bears no fruit, while every branch that does bear fruit he prunes so that it will be even more fruitful." (John 15:1-2)

We all experience hard times. Some of these are the result of stupid, sinful decisions. Those aren't too difficult to identify the source. Others occur because God wants to redirect our path. We have been heading in a certain direction, and for some reason, we didn't hear his whisper so he has to use more direct methods to get our attention.

And sometimes we experience hard times because we are walking closely with God and seeking to honor him in all we say and do.

Say what? That's right. Jesus uses the illustration of a vineyard to explain this aspect of spiritual life. When a gardener has a vine that produces a lot of grapes one year, he cuts it back at the beginning of the next year so it will produce even more. That's what pruning is all about. And that's what God does to you and me when we are serious about following him. He allows us to go through a difficult situation or a painful relationship to purify our motives and strengthen our faith. His attitude is like a coach who says, "You are doing great! In fact, you are doing so well that I think you're ready for the next level, so I'm giving you a more strenuous workout to get you in shape." Thanks, coach.

When you go through hard times, ask the Lord for insight about its cause. It may be from a dumb decision (or a bunch of them), it may be that God wants to get your attention, or it may be because you are doing so well that God wants to strengthen you even more. He's pruning you. Feel honored.

 Lord, prune me all you want because. . . .

 Think of the last time you struggled. What do you think was the source of the problem: sin, redirection, or pruning?

Read John 15:1-8

# Friends

> "I no longer call you servants, because a servant does not know his master's business. Instead, I have called you friends, for everything that I learned from my Father I have made known to you." (John 15:15-16)

What a moment in these guys lives! They had followed Jesus for over three years. They knew he was the Messiah, but they didn't understand a lot of the things he had told them. Now, when the chips were down and Jesus' enemies were closing in on him, he called these men aside and told them, "You guys are my closest friends. I trust you so much that I'm telling you my deepest secrets." That would be an honor coming from anybody, but coming from Jesus. . . . Wow!

And he calls you and me his friends, too.

Think about this: Jesus was the God of the universe who stepped out of eternity into time. He didn't need anything or anybody, but he humbled himself to become a friend to people who would reach back when he extended his hand.

Friends share their secret thoughts. Jesus told these men—and us—his greatest hopes and his greatest fears. I have a feeling that these guys felt safe enough to tell him absolutely anything about themselves.

We can, too.

It's a little hard to put the two together, isn't it? Creator and friend. God of the universe and confidant. (A confidant is someone you trust with your secrets.) But that's a part of the incredible grace of God. He doesn't love us from a distance. He loves us as our dearest friend.

And man, what a friend!

 Jesus, you call me your friend. That means the world to me because. . . .

☞ Tell Jesus your deepest, darkest secret. It's safe with him.

Read John 15:9-17

# Day 5 The War of the Worlds

"If the world hates you, keep in mind that it hated me first. If you belonged to the world, it would love you as its own. As it is, you do not belong to the world, but I have chosen you out of the world. That is why the world hates you." (John 15:18-19)

Jesus had just called his disciples his "friends." Now he gives the other side of the equation. If we are friends with Christ, we will be at war with the world. Jesus uses words like "love" and "hate" because this is serious business. We have to choose which world we belong to. We can't stay on the fence for long.

What does the world's hatred look like? In some countries, Christians are thrown into prison, tortured, and killed. Yes, it is happening today. One international agency says that Christians are persecuted more today than in any time in history. In this country, we are shielded from that kind of hatred, but we experience the more subtle forms of persecution. We are sometimes ignored, ridiculed, and laughed at by those who don't share our values or our love for God.

Some of us try to avoid the world's hatred by living two separate lives. When we are around Christians, we do the Jesus thing. But when we are with our nonChristian friends, we talk and act just like they do. This sends mixed messages to the world and actually hurts the cause of Christ. Hey, don't do that. Pick your pasture. Get off the fence. Either you are for Jesus or against him.

Jesus tells us that we can't stay on the fence because we don't belong to the world any more. We belong to him. He has chosen us. Individually. Because he loves you and me.

 Jesus, I want to be consistent in my heart. I don't want to live two lives. Help me. . . .

☞ Listen to "Be Glorified."

Read John 15:18-27

# End of the Week

<u>Looking up:</u>
Listen to "Be Glorified" and make it your prayer.

<u>Looking back:</u>
1. Which day's devotion and passage of Scripture meant the most to you this week? Explain:

2. How has God made his presence known to you (in your prayers, study of the Scriptures, in quiet moments, busy times, and in conversations)?

3. How have you seen God's hand at work in your circumstances and in the lives of others this week?

4. How have you responded to temptation, and what help did you find at the most difficult moments?

5. What fruit of the Spirit (Galatians 5:22-23) would you like to see increase in your life? (Love, Joy, Peace, Patience, Kindness, Goodness, Gentleness, Faithfulness, Self-control) What difference would this make in your attitude, relationships, etc?

6. What opportunities has God given you to serve others, and how did you respond?

7. Did God provide an opportunity for you to share your faith with someone? What happened?

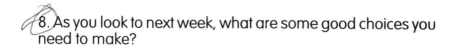

8. As you look to next week, what are some good choices you need to make?

In order to make those choices, Lord, I need you to. . . .

# THANK YOU

For all that You've done
I will thank You
For all that You're going to do
For all that You promised
And all that You are
Is all that has carried me through
Jesus, I thank You

And I thank You, thank You, Lord
And I thank You, I thank You, Lord

Thank You for loving and setting me free
Thank You for giving Your life just for me
How I thank You
Jesus, I thank You
Gratefully thank You
And I thank You

# Day 1 Guilt and Forgiveness

> "When [the Counselor] comes, he will convict the world of guilt in regard to sin and righteousness and judgment." (John 16:8)

If you are a Christian, it is because this verse has been fulfilled in your life. At some point, the light of the gospel shined on your sinful heart, and you became aware that you needed forgiveness. You also became aware that Jesus is the Messiah, the righteous Savior, and that his death on the cross is the only payment for sin. And too, at that moment you realized that you were escaping the judgment of God by embracing eternal life. These are some of the things the Holy Spirit—the Counselor—does for us.

The Holy Spirit is a fantastic gift from God. He (the Holy Spirit is not an it) is always at work to show men and women their need for a Savior. In our day, we wink too much at sin. We are entertained by it in the movies; we laugh at it among our friends. When I hear that someone is genuinely bent out of shape because they realize their sin is so awful, I am thrilled—not because I'm a sadist, but because that is a sign that the Holy Spirit is shining his light on the deepest parts of that person's life.

When we are thoroughly convinced of our sinfulness, we have a far deeper appreciation for our forgiveness . . . and for our Savior. As Jesus told people at a dinner once, "He who has been forgiven little loves little," but he who has been forgiven much loves much.

 Holy Spirit, thank you for pointing out sin so that I realize how much I am forgiven.

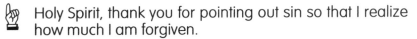 As you watch people today, notice when they are amused by sin. Pray that the Holy Spirit will convict them of sin, righteousness, and judgment.

Read John 16:1-16

# Good Grief

"So with you: Now is your time of grief, but I will see you again and you will rejoice, and no one will take away your joy." (John 16:22)

Jesus was going to die very soon. He knew it. He had told his guys a zillion times (OK, maybe not that many, but a lot!) that he was going to be killed, but they didn't want to believe it. Jesus anticipated the shock they were going to experience in the next few hours, so he gave them a promise: Yes, it will be really hard, but you will rejoice again later.

Nobody likes to grieve, but it's a part of life. We move away or a close friend moves away; a grandparent or parent dies; a friend gets very sick; a dream is shattered. Jesus didn't say, "Oh, get over it. Don't cry. It's no big deal." No, he told them to embrace their grief. As unpleasant as it is, face the reality of the loss. Feel sad. Recognize what you will miss.

But remember this: God has a purpose. He doesn't cause tragedies any more than God caused Jesus to go to the cross, but if we trust him and look for his hand at work, he has promised to use absolutely every thing for good in our lives (Romans 8:28). The situation itself may be awful, but at the very least, God will use the circumstance to deepen our dependence on him and give us new insights about his heart, his purposes, and his ways. Those are lessons that don't come easily. They only come from the school of grief. Nobody willingly enrolls there, but we all attend at one time or another.

Don't let your grief go to waste. Let God use it to deepen your faith in him.

 Jesus, show me your heart, your purposes, and your ways when I experience loss. Help me trust that you have good things for me even when I'm sad.

☞ Listen to "Thank You."

Read John 16:17-33

# Day 3    Eternal Life is Now!

> "Now this is eternal life: that they may know you, the only true God, and Jesus Christ, whom you have sent." (John 17:3)

We all imagine what heaven will be like: streets paved with gold, walls full of diamonds and emeralds and other jewels, gates made of pearl . . . and the ability to relate to Jesus face to face, to see his smile and hear his voice. That's eternal life!

But in his prayer before his death, Jesus gives us the startling insight that this kind of joy, this kind of fulfillment, and this kind of intimacy with him is available from the moment we receive Christ! He said, "This is eternal life," not "That will be eternal life."

I think we experience the presence of God just as much as we expect to. If we think we will only feel close to God on Sunday morning, then we probably won't have much awareness of him as we talk to friends on Tuesday night or take a biology exam on Friday. But if we realize that we can walk and talk with Jesus all day every day because he is always present to us, we will be much more likely to sense that he is there, depend on him at any and all moments of the day, and enjoy the constant companionship of our strong friend.

Listen to his voice as you read the Scriptures. Look for his hand at work in every conversation and every situation. Eternal life is the experience of God, and you can do that today, right now. Go for it!

 Lord Jesus, I can't see you, but I know you're here. . . .

 Look for God to be at work in every conversation and every situation today.

Read John 17:1-12

> "My prayer is not that you take them out of the world but that you protect them from the evil one. . . . As you sent me into the world, I have sent them into the world." (John 17:15, 18)

I have noticed something that happens in some youth groups that is not a good thing: they become their own clique at school, a "holy huddle" that isolates the people in the group from others. I can understand how that happens. We find love and forgiveness with these folks, and we want to spend as much time with them as possible. It makes sense. But when we become ingrown, we stop being light and salt to the world around us. Those people miss out on the great news we can share with them, and we miss out on the adventure of living a cutting edge faith.

Jesus said he has sent us into the world just like the Father sent him. That means we go:

—boldly, telling everybody who will listen about Jesus.

—confidently, knowing that God is at work in people's lives.

—realistically, certain that some will say "yes" and some will say "no" to Christ, and that the evil one wants to stop us any way he can.

—collectively, with others so we can support each other through all kinds of situations.

As you read the Gospel of John, notice that Jesus spent plenty of time with his disciples, but he always took them with him to accomplish his ultimate purpose: to seek and to save the lost.

Don't miss out on the adventure of seeing God use you to bring light to darkened hearts.

 Jesus, when I think of being "in the world but not of the world," I feel. . . .

 Grab a Christian friend and together tell someone today about Jesus.

Read John 17:13-19

# Day 5  Find Common Ground

"I have given them the glory that you gave me, that they may be one as we are one; I in them and you in me. May they be brought to complete unity to let the world know that you sent me and have loved them even as you have loved me." (John 17:22-23)

Many Christian groups exhibit a behavior that makes God very sad. We gripe and criticize and condemn each other in the group, and we do the same thing to other youth groups or groups on campus. Instead of non-Christians seeing the attractive love of Jesus, they are turned off by the ragging of his friends.

Why do we do that? I think it is because we are insecure. We feel like we have to be "one up" on somebody, so we put them down. They don't like it, and they rag us back . . . and it keeps going and going and. . . . Groups can have the attitude, "We're better than you." We compare the size of the group, how cool the leaders are, which camps we attend, and almost anything else just so we can find something to feel superior about. That stinks!

Unity doesn't mean agreement. Christians have disagreed on all kinds of things throughout church history. Many times, those disagreements have resulted in bitter hatred, and sometimes even murder. (Imagine how that makes God feel.) But I've also seen young people from different races, different denominations, and different countries come together in unity of purpose to honor Christ. It's a beautiful thing to see. They could find plenty of stuff to disagree about, but they overlook all those things for the sake of lifting up Jesus.

Go out of your way to overlook petty differences in your youth group or among groups on campus. Find common ground in the love of Christ.

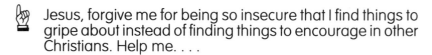 Jesus, forgive me for being so insecure that I find things to gripe about instead of finding things to encourage in other Christians. Help me. . . .

☞ Talk to a Christian from another youth group (preferably another race or another culture) today, and find common ground in Jesus.

Read John 17:20-26

# End of the Week

## Looking up:
Listen to "Thank You." Make it your prayer.

## Looking back:
1. Which day's devotion and passage of Scripture meant the most to you this week? Explain:

2. How has God made his presence known to you (in your prayers, study of the Scriptures, in quiet moments, busy times, and in conversations)?

3. How have you seen God's hand at work in your circumstances and in the lives of others this week?

4. How have you responded to temptation, and what help did you find at the most difficult moments?

5. What fruit of the Spirit (Galatians 5:22-23) would you like to see increase in your life? (Love, Joy, Peace, Patience, Kindness, Goodness, Gentleness, Faithfulness, Self-control)
What difference would this make in your attitude, relationships, etc?

6. What opportunities has God given you to serve others, and how did you
respond?

7. Did God provide an opportunity for you to share your faith with someone? What happened?

8. As you look to next week, what are some good choices you need to make?




In order to make those choices, Lord, I need you to. . . .

# UNENDING LOVE

How can I praise You enough
How can I show You the love
That You've shown to me
Jesus, You've healed a broken soul
And warmed the heart so cold
Opened my eyes so I can see . . .

Unending love
Abounding grace
You are the joy
Of all my days
I lift You up
I give You praise
For giving me
Unending love

# Drink the Cup

> Jesus commanded Peter, "Put your sword away! Shall I not drink the cup the Father has given me?" (John 18:11)

Peter didn't like the reality he saw: Jesus was being arrested. So Peter grabbed a sword and cut off the ear of a man in the crowd. (I don't think he was aiming for the guy's ear. Remember, Peter was a fisherman, not a soldier!) Jesus told him, "Pete, you don't get it. This is a part of the Father's plan for me . . . and for you, too. Take it easy, man . . . and pick up that guy's ear."

There are times I really like "the cup the Father has given me." I love seeing people respond to my music, and I love seeing my family grow. But sometimes I'm more like Peter. God shows me something he wants me to do, and I don't like it one bit. I get angry, and I try to change things any way I can. When I act this way, I make just as big a mess—and hurt people in the process—just like Peter.

What is the cup the Father has given you these days? Is it pleasant, or is it something you'd rather not drink? Maybe your parents are having problems in their marriage; maybe your dad got a new job and you'll have to move; maybe a trusted friend ditched you; or maybe the Holy Spirit has pointed out some area of your life he wants to change.

Self-pity and anger will only make your situation worse. Take the cup, ask God for wisdom and strength. And drink it. All of it.

 Jesus, the cup the Father has given me to drink these days is . . . .

☞ What happens when you don't "drink the cup the Father has given" you? . . . when you do?

Read John 18:1-14

# The Invisible Kingdom

Jesus said, "My kingdom is not of this world. If it were, my servants would fight to prevent my arrest by the Jews. But now my kingdom is from another place." (John 18:36)

Pilate figured out that Jesus was a king, but Jesus made it clear that his is an unseen kingdom. And the laws of his kingdom are very different than the physical world around us. If he had been an earthly king, soldiers would have fought to prevent his arrest. But Jesus knew that people could only become citizens of his unseen kingdom if he paid their entrance fee: his death.

We live in a very tangible world. Academics teach that we should value only those things we can see, taste, feel, and smell. But there is a parallel universe that is just as real—and much more powerful. That parallel universe has good guys and bad guys, angels and demons, who are at war around us right now.

As citizens of God's unseen kingdom, we have been given an incredible privilege and responsibility. We wear the sash of Christ's ambassadors to this earthly kingdom where we live. Paul wrote: "[God] has committed to us the message of reconciliation. We are therefore Christ's ambassadors, as though God were making his appeal through us. We implore you on Christ's behalf: Be reconciled to God."

As ambassadors, every word we say and every thing we do is scrutinized by the people of this earthly kingdom. We represent Jesus to them. They find out what he is like by watching us and listening to us. It is an awesome job, but we are not alone. We have constant communication with the king himself, and he has made every resource we could ever need available to us.

Be confident. Be bold. You represent Christ's unseen kingdom to people who need to change their citizenship.

 Lord, when I think of being your ambassador, it makes me feel. . . .

 Write down your observations: How does an ambassador relate to people in the country were he is assigned? How does he relate to his king?

Read John 18:15-40

# At the End

> Near the cross of Jesus stood his mother, his mother's sister, Mary the wife of Clopas, and Mary Magdalene. When Jesus saw his mother there, and the disciple whom Jesus loved standing nearby, he said to his mother, "Dear woman, here is your son." (John 19:25-26)

Earlier in John, we read about Jesus healing the sick and raising the dead. He fed the 5000 (but that included only the men, so the number was probably 15-20,000 people in all). He was enormously popular—until he started calling people to a commitment. At that point, most of them left him. They enjoyed all the benefits and the entertainment, but they didn't want to change their lives.

In that last week or so of his life, Jesus was followed only by a small group of people: his disciples and a few women. Then one of his own guys betrayed him. When he was arrested, all the rest ran away and hid. None stayed with him—except John. By the time we see Jesus hanging in pain on the cross, we find only four women and John.

Would you have been there? Would I?

It's easy to hang out with Christians when the skits are fun and everybody is hugging each other. But who will stand up for Christ when a teacher laughs at the resurrection or a friend walks away because we have trusted Christ.

Each of us have tests along the way to strengthen our faith. The good news is that each of the disciples got stronger from this test. Each of them stayed strong for the rest of their lives.

If you had been one of the disciples or one of the women who followed Jesus, would you have been there at the end?

☞ Jesus, I want to be there for you when the chips are down. . . .

☞ Listen to "Unending Love." How are you responding these days to Jesus' unending love?

Read John 19:1-27

# Paid in Full

> When he had received the drink, Jesus said, "It is finished."
> With that, he bowed his head and gave up his spirit.
> (John 19:30)

In the Greek translations of the New Testament, the word for "It is finished" is tetelestei. It means "paid in full." Jesus' purpose for coming to earth was to be the Suffering Savior, to pay for the sins of men and women, you and me. He didn't make a down payment and expect us to pay more later. He paid it all. Nothing can be added. We insult him if we think we can do something to earn forgiveness. We simply accept it as a free gift.

It is free, but it was incredibly expensive—free to us; expensive to Jesus.

Sometimes I hear someone say, "Well, hey, if God's grace is free, I can sin all I want! I'm still forgiven." That person doesn't have a clue about grace.

Imagine being on death row facing immediate execution. A man walks in and says, "Stop! Don't kill that person." The jailor replies, "He is guilty. He deserves to die." The intruder calmly states, "Take me instead. Set him free." The jailors talk about it for a minute, then one of them answers, "OK, you're on. Get on this gurney and roll up your sleeve." They take the handcuffs off you and show you the door. "You're free to go." And the man is put to death.

How would you feel about this man who saved your life? Wouldn't you be gripped with the deepest thankfulness for what he had done to you? Wouldn't you tell everybody you see about his incredible kindness to you? Wouldn't you tell his family how much you appreciate his sacrifice? Wouldn't you live your life in a way that reflects your thankfulness?

Then do it.

 Jesus, your grace is free, but it cost you a lot. Thank you. . . .

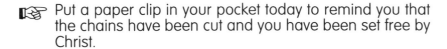 Put a paper clip in your pocket today to remind you that the chains have been cut and you have been set free by Christ.

Read John 19:28-30

# Day 5  Overwhelming Proof

> The man who saw it has given testimony, and his testimony is true. He knows that he tells the truth, and he testifies so that you also may believe. These things happened so that the scripture would be fulfilled. . . . (John 19:35-36)

Our confidence in the Bible is not just that it is a nice book with nice stories about some nice people. One of the things that gives us confidence that it is, indeed, God's word are all the prophecies which are fulfilled. The Old Testament contains over 300 specific prophecies about the Messiah who would come: where he would be born, what Jewish tribe he would be from, his ministry of healing the sick and making blind people see, and his betrayal by a friend. Regarding his death, we find many specific predictions: his clothes would be gambled for; he would be beaten savagely; he would suffocate to death; his body would be pierced; a rich man would take his lifeless body and bury it; the Messiah would be raised from the dead in three days.

A mathematician calculated that the odds of 8 of these 300 being fulfilled in one man to be 1 X 10 to the 17th power. That's a lot of zeroes! And the odds on 20 of them are so high that it's hard to grasp the number. To think of the odds of one person fulfilling all 300 . . . well, it takes far greater faith to believe that Jesus isn't the Messiah than to believe that he is!

I'm glad God put those prophecies in the Bible to strengthen our faith—and to amaze us that he is a God of incredible detail. He loves us enough (and he knows that our doubts sometimes need to be countered with truth) to give us overwhelming evidence of prophecies that Jesus is the Messiah.

They convinced John.

And they convince me.

 Lord, thank you for all the prophecies which have been fulfilled. That gives me confidence to trust you to. . . .

 Read Psalm 22. It was written by David 1000 years before Jesus lived. Notice the incredible detail about the crucifixion of the Messiah.

Read John 19:31-42

# End of the Week

## Looking up:
Listen to "Unending Love" and make it a prayer.

## Looking back:
1. Which day's devotion and passage of Scripture meant the most to you this week? Explain:

2. How has God made his presence known to you (in your prayers, study of the Scriptures, in quiet moments, busy times, and in conversations)?

3. How have you seen God's hand at work in your circumstances and in the lives of others this week?

4. How have you responded to temptation, and what help did you find at the most difficult moments?

5. What fruit of the Spirit (Galatians 5:22-23) would you like to see increase in your life? (Love, Joy, Peace, Patience, Kindness, Goodness, Gentleness, Faithfulness, Self-control)
What difference would this make in your attitude, relationships, etc?

6. What opportunities has God given you to serve others, and how did you respond?'

7. Did God provide an opportunity for you to share your faith with someone? What happened?

8. As you look to next week, what are some good choices you need to make?

In order to make those choices, Lord, I need you to. . . .

# ALL I CAN SAY

Lord, I am tired and weary
Worn by the weight of this life
But I know that You are here with me
And You're drawing me close to Your side
And You carry me into Your shelter
You cover me under Your love
Under Your love

And all I can say is I love You
More and more every day
I will rest in Your shadow forever
Father, I love You, Father, I love You
And all I can say is I'll trust You
Step by step all of the way
You will abandon me never
Father, I love You, Father, I love You

Father I do

# Day 1    Seeing is Believing

> Then Simon Peter . . . arrived and went into the tomb. . . . Finally the other disciple, who had reached the tomb first, also went inside. He saw and believed. (John 20:6,8)

Peter and John ran to the tomb. John stopped at the entrance, but Peter ran past him inside. There they found the linen grave clothes laying empty, and the cloth which had been around Jesus' head folded neatly to the side. They saw the evidence. And they believed.

The disciples had all kinds of tangible, physical evidence. When John begins his first letter, he writes, "That which was from the beginning, which we have heard, which we have seen with our eyes, which we have looked at and our hands have touched—this we proclaim concerning the Word of life."

We get it straight from these eyewitnesses. We read what they wrote. We listen to what they said. And we believe, too.

But God also gives us evidence. As we walk with God and put ourselves around people who trust God to work, we see lives changed. We don't see Jesus' actual grave cloths like Peter and John saw, but we see evidences of the power of the resurrected Christ. Dark-hearted people experience forgiveness. The hearts of bitter people are melted by love. Broken relationships are mended. Wanderers find direction. Deep emotional wounds are healed.

These are the things you and I see and touch and hear. And we believe even more. Are you seeing God change lives? Find people who are serious about experiencing the power and presence of Christ, and ask God, "What do you want to do here, Lord?"

He wants to show himself. Again and again.

 Jesus, I want to see and feel and touch and taste your power and presence. Open my eyes to. . . .

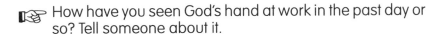 How have you seen God's hand at work in the past day or so? Tell someone about it.

Read John 20:1-9

# Presence and Purpose

> Again Jesus said, "Peace be with you! As the Father has sent me. I am sending you." (John 20:21)

Why do you think Jesus talked so much to the disciples about peace? I think it was because they were filled with so much fear. One of the greatest fear producers in life is change—and Jesus had turned their world upside down! They left their homes; they followed a radical teacher; that teacher had been attacked by the religious leaders; and then he had been killed. They had been a bunch of fishermen, tax collectors, and other blue-collar workers. Now Jesus was asking them to change jobs. He was sending them out to tell the whole world about him. Talk about change!

Where does this peace come from? Jesus assured them of two things: "I will be with you," and "You have the same sense of purpose I received from the Father." Peace comes from Jesus' presence and his purpose. When we are afraid, we need to remember that he is right here with us, and too, he has entrusted us with the greatest mission in all of history: to represent him to anybody and everybody. If our purpose is to honor Christ, we can accomplish that goal no matter what situation we are in.

Think about those two things next time you feel afraid or lost—and the God of peace will be with you.

 Jesus, thank you for your peace. I want to honor you today in this circumstance. . . .

 Listen to "All I Can Say."

Read John 20:10-23

# Day 3   Jesus' Persistence

Then he said to Thomas, "Put your finger here; see my hands. Reach out your hand and put it into my side. Stop doubting and believe."

Thomas said to him, "My Lord and my God!" (John 20:27-28)

I'm really glad John included this story about Thomas. Thomas was a skeptic. He had a hard time believing what he didn't see with his own eyes and feel with his own hands. A lot of us are just like him!

Thomas had been with Jesus for over three years. He had seen countless people healed of diseases and raised from the dead. He had observed Jesus cast out demons, walk on water, and calm storms at sea. He had been so close he could touch each person in each situation.

But still he doubted.

Just a moment before Jesus spoke to Thomas in John 20, an amazing thing happened. John wrote, "Though the doors were locked, Jesus came and stood among them. . . ." Do what!? Jesus appeared in the room like Captain Kirk being beamed aboard the Enterprise! He just appeared out of nowhere.

But still Thomas doubted.

Now Jesus approached him. He asked Thomas to touch the nail holes in his hands and the spear hole in his side. Thomas touched him, and finally, he believed.

The thing that encourages me about this is that Jesus kept pursuing Thomas to convince him. What discourages me is that Thomas missed out on the benefits of believing for so long.

 Jesus, I'm like Thomas when. . . . Thank you for convincing me.

 Write the words "Whatever it takes" on a piece of paper and put it in your pocket. Remember today that Jesus does whatever it takes to convince us of his love and power.

Read John 20:24-31

# Get Back Up!

The third time he said to him, "Simon, son of John, do you love me?" (John 21:17)

Peter had blown it. Big time. He had been the leader of Jesus' band of disciples, the spokesman, the one who the others looked to. Toward the end when Jesus told them he was to be killed because he was being betrayed by one of them, Peter confidently said he would never fail him.

Then he denied even knowing Jesus. To a little girl.

I wonder what it was like for Peter during those days: hearing the crowd jeer Jesus on the road to the cross, seeing darkness fall in the middle of the day as Jesus died, the long weekend of hiding and grieving, the incredible news that Jesus was alive. Then he was told that Jesus wanted to see him. I think Peter's heart was pounding as he waited for Jesus to speak.

Jesus didn't lecture Peter. He didn't ask the dreaded "Why?" question. (I think Peter may have been ready for that one.) Jesus simply asked him three questions. Well, actually he asked him the same question three times: "Peter, do you love me?"

Each time, Peter swallowed hard and said, "Yes, Lord, you know I love you." Three times Peter denied Christ. Jesus gave Peter three opportunities to reaffirm his love for him. Perfect symmetry.

When we fail, I believe God gives us opportunities to re-affirm our love and commitment to him, usually in the same way we failed. These are a part of his grace to us to let us play a part in climbing back where we need to be.

When you fail in your faith, look for Christ to give you an opportunity to reaffirm your commitment. And be thankful.

 Jesus, thank you that you give me opportunities to get up when I fall. . . .

☞ Use to "All I Can Say" as a prayer.

Read John 21:1-19

# Day 5     Just for You

> Peter turned and saw that the disciple whom Jesus loved was following them. When Peter saw him, he asked, "Lord, what about him?" (John 21:20-21)

God doesn't necessarily have the same plan in mind for any two people, even two people who have been through a lot of things together. That was true of Peter and John. It is true of you and your friends, too. Jesus answer to Peter's question was, "Don't worry about him. You follow me." He has the same message for you and me today.

God gives each of us different gifts, different abilities, and different opportunities. To some degree, our responses to the choices God gives us take us down life's path. But ultimately, it is God's path for each of us, not a path we can choose ourselves. He is our Lord, our Master. It isn't smart or proper for a servant to say to his master, "Hey, I don't like the job you've given me! I want another one." A wise servant gladly accepts the responsibilities and the life the Master gives.

In our case, our Master loves us more than any human could, and his path for each of us is more exciting than we can imagine. He will give some of us relatively smooth sailing, but he will take some of us through the rocky mountains of tragedy and disappointment. It's not that he loves one more than another. But it may be that he knows some of us have stronger character than some others.

Don't desire a life of ease, and don't compare God's plan for you to his plan for someone else. Determine to follow God no matter what path he chooses for you. It's the greatest adventure of your life.

 Lord Jesus, I want to walk the path you've chosen for me. Strengthen me. . . .

☞ Take some time alone today. Ask God for a vision of how he might want to use you in other's lives.

Read John 21:20-25

# HOLINESS

Holiness, holiness is what I long for
Holiness, holiness is what I need
Holiness, holiness is what You want from me

Take my heart and form it
Take my mind, transform it
Take my will, conform it
To Yours, to Yours O Lord

Brokenness, brokenness is what I long for
Brokenness, brokenness  is what I need
Brokenness, brokenness is what You want from me

# End of the Week

## <u>Looking up:</u>
Listen to "Holiness" and make it your prayer.

## <u>Looking back:</u>
1. Which day's devotion and passage of Scripture meant the most to you this week? Explain:

2. How has God made his presence known to you (in your prayers, study of the Scriptures, in quiet moments, busy times, and in conversations)?

3. How have you seen God's hand at work in your circumstances and in the lives of others this week?

4. How have you responded to temptation, and what help did you find at the most difficult moments?

5. What fruit of the Spirit (Galatians 5:22-23) would you like to see increase in your life? (Love, Joy, Peace, Patience, Kindness, Goodness, Gentleness, Faithfulness, Self-control) What difference would this make in your attitude, relationships, etc?

6. What opportunities has God given you to serve others, and how did you respond?

7. Did God provide an opportunity for you to share your faith with someone? What happened?

8. As you look to next week, what are some good choices you need to make?

In order to make those choices, Lord, I need you to. . . .

About the Authors:

# Joel Engle

Joel Engle was born in San Francisco. His father left home when he was only one month old, and his mother died suddenly when Joel was eleven. He was sent to live with his elderly grandparents in Oklahoma, but when Joel was fifteen, his grandfather died. Shortly after that, Joel put himself in the Oklahoma City Baptist Children's Home. One year later, he was adopted by the Engle family, who introduced Joel to the father he never had: Jesus Christ.

For the last ten years, Joel has traveled throughout the United States, singing and speaking about the love of Jesus and his power to change lives. Joel's passion is to see students' lives transformed by the reality of Jesus Christ. In 1997, Joel and his wife Valerie started a music company called SPIN, which helps almost a hundred thousand students praise God each week.

Joel and Valerie live in Fort Worth, Texas, where they are involved with First Baptist Church of Euless.

# Pat Springle

Pat Springle was on the staff of Campus Crusade for Christ for eighteen years, and for eleven of those years, he served as the Texas Area Director. He was Senior Vice President of Rapha Treatment Centers for three years, then he became the President of Baxter Press. Pat has authored or co-authored more than thirty books. He and his wife Joyce have two children, Catherine and Taylor. They live in Friendswood, Texas.

# Want More Great Music?

Joel has recorded several worship and praise releases designed to encourage your heart and lift your spirit. Take a look. . . .

## Surrender

This album is Joel's best-selling collection of songs out right now: ten of his best original songs in a totally modern, "edgy" style. Two very popular songs from this album include "I Run To You" and "You Are The Holy One." Your ears and your soul will love every song on this album!

## Unending Love

This CD is a terrific combination of some of Joel's best original songs and some of his most popular praise concert songs—a very strong mixture of the best in praise and worship!

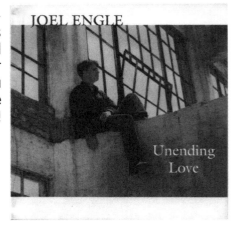

# The Father I Never Had

Originally produced as a radio demo, this CD features two versions of Joel's "testimony song," "The Father I Never Had," plus Joel shares about his testimony, how the song came about, and about his ministry on this CD. The price of this one is only $10 since it is a single-song CD.

## Wrap Your Arms Around Me

This CD features songs about healing, such as the title song and "All I Can Say," plus much more including originals from Joel as well as him singing two of his favorite Dennis Jernigan tunes, "We Will Worship" and "All in All."

And you may want more copies of

## Glorify

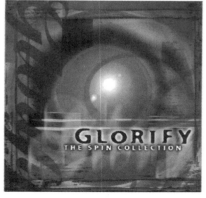

This CD is a compilation of sixteen of the best praise and worship songs from SPIN, the Student Praise Interactive Network, Joel's music company that sends cutting-edge worship resources to student ministers worldwide every quarter. This CD features lots of favorite upbeat tunes such as "Every Move I Make" and three tunes by Delerious, plus some "new classics" such as "Open The Eyes Of My Heart" and "Be Glorified."

# Prices

Surrender ................................. CD $15
                                        Cassette $10

Unending Love ........................ CD $15
                                        Cassette $10

The Father I Never Had ........... CD $10

Wrap Your Arms Around Me .. CD $15
                                        Cassette $10

Glorify ....................................... Book & CD $17.95
                                        CD $15
                                        Cassette $10

# Order Form

| Title | Quantity | CD/Cassette/Set Price each | Total |
|-------|----------|----------------------------|-------|
|       |          |                            |       |
|       |          |                            |       |
|       |          |                            |       |
|       |          |                            |       |

Tax and shipping are included in the price.

Grand Total _____

**Payment**
___check
___Visa
___MasterCard
___Discover
___AmEx

**Credit card #**

☐☐☐☐☐☐☐☐☐☐☐☐☐☐☐☐

**Expiration date**

☐☐  ☐☐
Month   Year

_____
Signature

A printed receipt from our credit card terminal will be sent with all credit card orders for your records.

SHIP TO: Name _____

Mailing Address _____

City, State & ZIP _____

Mail this order form and your payment to:
Joel Engle Ministries
4821 Great Divide Drive
Ft. Worth, TX 76137-5130

Or if you are paying by credit card. . . .
—you can call in your order: (888) 697-7746, 9 am to 3:30 pm
Central Time
—or fax it in: (817) 337-0954

Are you looking for a resource that puts the latest praise and worship music in your hands to use in your group meetings?

You've Found It!

## The Student Praise Interactive Network

SPIN is a yearly subscription for student ministers or student worship leaders, providing you with the BEST new praise and worship songs from Delerious to Passion!

## As a subscriber to SPIN, every three months you get a packet of worship resources, including:

- demonstrated tracks on CD (the Glorify CD is a collection of demonstrated tracks taken straight from SPIN CD's)
- instrumental tracks on CD,
- chord charts to all the songs,
- sheet music to all the songs,
- overheads ready to use with the lyrics,
- lyrics on Power Point (on 3.5" disk), and
- a newsletter full of great ideas!

"These CD's have revolutionized our worship time! SPIN is such a versatile tool for our ministry! Our students learn it fast and we have a great variety to choose from. It's well worth the investment— both  time and money!"
Jeff Gilliam, Seminole, Texas

## Sign Me Up!

A one-year subscription (four packets with all of the above) is only $149.95 plus $12.80 shipping, for a total of $162.75.

A subscription begins with the most current packet and goes on from there. Subscribers can get any earlier SPIN packets for just $25 including shipping on the day they subscribe or for just $30 including shipping anytime later. (Non subscribers pay $42 plus $3.20 shipping for any packet, current or past.)

# SPIN Order Form

Please ship my quarterly packets to:

Name _____

Church Name _____

Mailing Address _____

_____

City, State & ZIP _____

Phone _____

• Circle one: this address is my   home   or   church.

• Do you want the lyrics on a 3.5" disk as well as transparancies?
If yes, circle:  PC  or  Mac (no extra charge)

Total enclosed: _____

Payment                    Credit card #

____check

____Visa

____MasterCard                    Expiration date

____Discover

____AmEx                            Month    Year

_____
Signature

A printed receipt from our credit card terminal will be sent with all credit
card orders for your records.

Mail this order form and your payment to:
**Joel Engle Ministries**
**4821 Great Divide Drive**
**Ft. Worth, TX 76137-5130**

Or if you are paying by credit card. . . .
—you can call in your order: (888) 697-7746, 9 am to 3:30 pm
Central Time
—or fax it in: (817) 337-0954

SPIN comes with a money-back  guarantee: If you don't like it,
return it within 30 days for a full refund!

## To Schedule Joel . . .

Joel is in great demand as a worship leader and speaker. To schedule him for your church, area-wide event, or camp, call:

(817) 377-1681

## Check Us Out on the Web!

See what's going on in Joel's ministry. Find us at:

www.spin360.com